Women: A Bibliography
of Bibliographies

*A
Reference
Publication
in
Women's
Studies*

Barbara Haber
Editor

Women: A Bibliography of Bibliographies

PATRICIA K. BALLOU

G.K.HALL&CO.

70 LINCOLN STREET, BOSTON, MASS.

HQ
1121
B32
1980

Library of Congress Cataloging in Publication Data

Ballou, Patricia K
  Women, a bibliography of bibliographies.

  Includes index.
  1. Bibliography--Bibliography--Women. I. Title.
Z7961.A1B34 [HQ1121]   016.0163054   80-21042
ISBN 0-8161-8292-2

This publication is printed on permanent/durable acid-free paper
MANUFACTURED IN THE UNITED STATES OF AMERICA

Contents

Contents

Contents

Contents

Introduction

The bibliographies listed in this book are concerned primarily with women or with a topic traditionally associated with women. In literary form they include annotated and unannotated lists of citations, bibliographic essays, literature reviews, library catalogs, and guides to archives or manuscript repositories. The format may be a whole book, part of a book, pamphlet, journal article, or microform. Imprint dates are from 1970 through 1979; some works listed were still forthcoming in November 1979. Although the materials cited in a bibliography may be in English or in foreign languages, English is always one of the editorial languages used, the only exception being Canadian bibliographies in French.

Certain types of bibliography are excluded: those dealing with one or several individuals; lists of nonsexist children's books, nonprint media, or professional medical literature; auction or antiquarian book dealers' catalogs; reprints of works first issued before 1970. Newsletters of the women's caucuses of academic disciplines are also not included. While they are an outstanding source of information on new publications and work in progress, their addresses change too often to make an accurate listing possible.

This is a selective bibliography, more selective than I anticipated when I began work on it. Whatever the reasons may be--the interdisciplinary nature of women's studies, the compensatory element in research on women, the tradition of sharing that endures among feminist scholars--the flood of literature on women produced over the last ten years has been recorded in a remarkable number of bibliographies. I have chosen the ones listed here after weighing their scope, availability, organization, and commentary. Few bibliographies of less than fifty items are included, and few that I know to be out of print. Bibliographies with a topical arrangement or a subject index have been given preference over those of similar scope that only list entries alphabetically, and annotated bibliographies or literature reviews have been preferred over mere citation lists. I have included bibliographies compiled and annotated from a feminist perspective, even when their content has been relatively slight, because of the special contribution made by their viewpoint. (Had I discovered any admittedly sexist bibliographies, I would have felt that they, too, were of special value.)

Introduction

I urge you to read through the Table of Contents to locate the sections that apply to the subject of your research. Each citation appears only once, in the subject section where I believe it is most useful, with cross-references to other sections where it might logically appear. Bibliographies on a topical subject within a specific geographical area other than the United States are listed among geographical subjects, with a cross-reference under topic. Bibliographies dealing with a group of women sharing a common social characteristic such as race, age, marital status, or sexual preference are grouped together as subsections of "Sociology." This decision was a pragmatic one based on my experience of the way people use library materials.

The choice of section headings, on the other hand, is a declaration of principle. I have used headings from Joan K. Marshall's On Equal Terms: A Thesaurus for Nonsexist Indexing and Cataloging whenever one was available. There is one exception: since the titles in the section "Black Women" use that term, I have gone along with them.

All but 28 of the 557 citations in this volume are annotated. Annotations for published items are based on my own examination; those for works still forthcoming state the source of information. Quoted matter in an annotation is taken from the introductory portion of the bibliography described. If neither the title of a bibliography nor the annotation describes it as annotated, it is not. Information provided in a title is not repeated in the annotation unless it calls for comment. Finally, although objectivity has been my goal, I have discovered that the line between a descriptive annotation and an evaluative one is narrow indeed, and I have not always been able to suppress a note of exasperation or enthusiasm.

Because of their reliable availability as well as their content, I have included a number of titles from three data bases (ERIC, NTIS, JSAS) that publish research reports and other documents on microfiche.

ERIC (Educational Resources Information Center) documents are cited in this bibliography as "Available from EDRS" followed by an ED number. Full order information is given in Resources in Education; order from ERIC Document Reproduction Service, P.O. Box 190, Arlington, VA 22210.

NTIS (National Technical Information Service) documents are cited here as "Available from NTIS" followed by one of a variety of letter/number combinations. The source of full order information is Government Reports Announcement, and the mailing address is National Technical Information Service, 5285 Port Royal Road, Springfield, VA 22161.

JSAS (Journal Supplement Abstract Service) manuscripts are cited by their abstracts in Catalog of Selected Documents in Psychology, followed by the MS number. Full order information is given in the Catalog; the mailing address is Journal Supplement Abstract Service, American Psychological Association, 1200 17th Street NW, Washington, D.C. 20036.

Introduction

Any bibliography begins to be out of date as soon as it is fin-
ished. I have tried to offset this problem by including all the
continuing bibliographies I could find. Item numbers for these are
preceded by *. Some of them are serial bibliographies devoted solely
to a woman-related topic, for example *417, <u>Marriage and Family Review</u>.
Others are bibliographies on broader topics that regularly contain a
section on women, for example *459, <u>Current Literature on Aging</u>. To
present an intelligible entry in such cases, I have written the citation for the whole publication rather than for the part, but each of
these recurring sections amounts to a serial bibliography on women
in its subject area, and in no instance have I listed a continuing
bibliography in which "women" must be used as an index term.

Patricia K. Ballou

Acknowledgments

Although I take full responsibility for errors and omissions in this volume and will appreciate having them called to my attention, I must also acknowledge the great assistance I have received from other librarians and colleagues. My thanks go out to all the persons who responded to questionnaires or inquiries and especially to Jeanne Audrey Powers of the Commission on the Status and Role of Women of the United Methodist Church and Deborah Edel of Lesbian Herstory Archives, each of whom shared with me her knowledge of the bibliographies in her subject area.

The unique position of Barnard College as an institution dedicated to women's education and associated with a great university has given me access to invaluable library resources. Although space does not permit me to list all the librarians at Barnard College and Columbia University who have been helpful, I must put on record my debt to Eileen McIlvaine of Butler Library Reference Department, Diane Goon of Lehman Library Reference Department, Bryan May of the Documents Service Center, and Mary Ellen Tucker, Barnard Acquisitions Librarian, all of whom have kept my interests in mind over the long haul. The staff of the Barnard Women's Center have earned my gratitude for both their resource collection and their warm encouragement.

This work has grown out of a review essay published in Signs in 1977. I am indebted to Catharine Stimpson and other members of the editorial staff for their confidence in me, their counsel--and their review copies.

My deepest thanks go to my husband.

Bibliographies

General and Interdisciplinary

*001   GÖTEBORG. Universitetsbibliotek. Kvinnohistoriskt Arkiv.
       Förteckning over Nyutkommen Litteratur. Göteborg:
       1972(?)-Quarterly.
          Issued by the Women's History Archives, established in
       1958 and since 1971 part of the Göteborg University Library,
       this is an international serial bibliography of current
       materials dealing with the history of women, including
       women today. Its topical arrangement is alphabetical by
       the Swedish form of the subject heading, with a prelimi-
       nary list providing English translations. (Since "Sverige"
       does not appear among the place names listed, the substan-
       tial amount of material on women in Sweden must be sought
       under its topical subjects.) This tool has its chief value
       for North Americans in its international coverage, espe-
       cially for European titles.

002   HUGHES, MARIJA MATICH. The Sexual Barrier: Legal, Medical,
      Economic and Social Aspects of Sex Discrimination. Washing-
      ton: Hughes Press, 1977. 843 pp.
         This massive interdisciplinary bibliography of 8,000
      items lists, with brief annotations, English language books,
      articles, pamphlets, and documents published from 1960
      through 1975, including some reprints of nineteenth century
      titles. The revised and enlarged version of an earlier
      edition subtitled "Legal and Economic Aspects of Employment,"
      it is notably strong in those subject areas and in the
      social sciences generally. It is less useful for some
      newly added topics from the humanities such as religion and
      history, and much of the large amount of medical literature
      is very technical. Arrangement is in seventeen subject
      chapters subdivided in detail. Author index.

003   JACOBS, SUE-ELLEN. Women in Perspective: A Guide for Cross-
      Cultural Studies. Urbana: University of Illinois Press,
      1974. 299 pp.

3

Compiled by an anthropologist as a contribution to the
cross-cultural analysis of women by the behavioral sciences
in general as well as by anthropology, this selective ret-
rospective bibliography of books and articles reflects the
compiler's interests in its organization and emphasis.
Part 1, the longer section, is organized geographically by
continent and country. Part 2, less useful, covers a wide
assortment of topics related to women in general, from
primate studies to women's studies publications. Few
titles from the geographical section are repeated under
topic. Author index.

004 KRICHMAR, ALBERT. The Women's Movement in the Seventies: An
International English-Language Bibliography. Metuchen,
N.J.: Scarecrow Press, 1977. 875 pp.
The emphasis of this bibliography is on worldwide "change,
attempted change, and continuing problems confronting women,"
and its scope is as broad topically as it is geographically.
The 8,637 references represent books, dissertations, pamphlets, research reports, periodical articles, and documents
published between 1970 and early 1976 in any country for
which bibliographic data were available. (Materials on the
U.S. are understandably prominent.) About 60 percent of
the titles have brief annotations. The work is organized
geographically with subject divisions as the literature on
a region or country warrants, the possible subjects including general works, culture and literature, economics,
education, law and politics, psychology, religion and philosophy, science and technology, sociology and anthropology.
There are also a chapter on reference books (a good source
of bibliographies) and author and subject indexes.

005 OAKES, ELIZABETH H. and SHELDON, KATHLEEN. Guide to Social
Science Resources in Women's Studies. Santa Barbara,
Calif.: ABC-Clio, 1978. 162 pp.
This book lists 654 monographs, anthologies, women's
studies periodicals, and special issues of other periodicals, all in English and mostly written in the 1970s. Selec-
Selection is based on frequent citation or recent publication
and on interdisciplinary and international focus. The
substantial annotations describe each work's scope and
thesis and evaluate its usefulness for undergraduates. The
chapter topics include anthropology, economics, history,
psychology, sociology, feminist thought, bibliographies,
journals, and other resources. There are author and subject
indexes.

*006 Resources for Feminist Research/Documentation sur la recherche
féministe. (Formerly Canadian Newsletter of Research on
Women/Recherches sur la femme: Bulletin d'information
canadien.) vol. 1- 1972- Quarterly.

In reporting current research on women and sex roles, this international journal places primary emphasis on Canadian research and subject matter, gives strong representation to British and western European work, and deliberately excludes U.S. materials except for bibliographies, periodicals, and other means of access to American scholarship. Its regular features have included abstracts of published research and work in progress--book reviews, bibliographies, reports of archival holdings, syllabi for women's studies courses, and conference reports. Two noteworthy sections are devoted to men's studies and special issues of periodicals.

*007   Resources In Women's Educational Equity. vol. 1- Washington: Dept. of Health, Education, and Welfare, Office of Education. For sale by the Supt. of Docs., U.S. Govt. Print. Off. 1977- Annual. (Cover title: Women's Educational Equity Communications Network. Resources in Women's Educational Equity.)
    Each volume of this sizable continuing bibliography is a compilation of well over 1,000 abstracts retrieved by computer search of a broad series of data bases (8 in 1977, 13 in 1979). The subject categories used in the search include not only education but also law, careers, sex differences, life style, and health, making it a valuable general tool. Arrangement is by data base, each section preceded by instructions for ordering the documents cited, and there are author, subject, and institutional indexes. As of July 1979, documents entered into data bases from 1976 through October 1978 have been covered, and both a retrospective volume and a further current volume have been announced for fall 1979.

008   ROSENBERG, MARIE BAROVIC and BERGSTROM, LEN V. Women and Society: A Critical Review of the Literature with a Selected Annotated Bibliography. Beverly Hills, Calif.: Sage Publications, 1975. 354 pp.
    The critical review is a twenty-one page bibliographic essay on women in history, at work, and in politics. The bibliography consists of close to 4,000 citations to authoritative and available scholarly books, journals, pamphlets, and articles on women in cross-cultural perspective. The presence of many older works, both European and American, is a strong point: writings listed range in date from Plato to 1974 and, while mostly in English, include a number in foreign languages. A detailed subject arrangement of 11 sections with 63 subsections makes it possible to find mini-bibliographies on very specific subjects. Annotations are brief and should be used with caution. Four indexes: Author/organization, Journal issues on women, Persons not cited as authors, Places/subjects. Continued by:

009   EEN, JOANN DELORES and ROSENBERG-DISHMAN, MARIE B. Women and
      Society: Citations 3601 to 6000: An Annotated Bibliography.
      Beverly Hills, Calif.: Sage Publications, 1978. 277 pp.
         With minor exceptions this work follows the same prin-
      ciples of selection and organization as the preceding
      volume, citing an additional 2,400 titles published from
      February 1974 through 1976 (including reprints of earlier
      works) plus some items omitted from the first volume.

      STINEMAN, ESTHER. Women's Studies: A Recommended Core Bibli-
      ography. Littleton, Colo.: Libraries Unlimited, 1979.
      670 pp.
         The intent of this bibliography is "to provide an anno-
      tated and indexed collection, organized around traditional
      disciplines, of English-language, mainly in-print publica-
      tions" to support an undergraduate women's studies curricu-
      lum. The compiler's forthright feminism is evident in intro-
      duction and annotations, but she has tried to include in her
      selection as many viewpoints as she can and still have it a
      core collection. The annotations give not only the content
      and arrangement of a work but also its value for women's
      studies and its relation to other books on similar topics.
      (The mention of these other works means that the bibliography
      actually covers many more titles than its 1,763 numbered
      entries would indicate.) Most of the twenty-six chapters
      deal with a specific subject area, but there are also four
      chapters on reference books of different types and one on
      periodicals. Author, title, and subject indexes conclude
      the volume.

011   UNITED NATIONS. Dag Hammarskjold Library. Status of Women:
      A Select Bibliography/Condition de la femme: Bibliographie
      selective. White Plains, N.Y.: UNIFO Publishers, 1976.
      121 pp.
         This international bibliography was prepared as the
      Library's contribution to the documentation for the 1975
      Conference of the International Women's Year and is made
      up principally of books and articles appearing during the
      previous ten years. Titles are given in the original lan-
      guage; subject headings and other editorial apparatus are
      in both English and French. The work is structured by
      broad subjects (Women in society; Women in Islam; Political
      participation; Employment and related economic roles; Women
      in professions; Education and training; Legal status includ-
      ing family law; Women and the family; Women and population)
      with each topical section further divided by continent and
      country. Two final sections list major UN documents and
      other bibliographies.

*012 Women Studies Abstracts. Rush, N.Y.: Rush Publishing Co.
      vol. 1- 1972- Quarterly.

This is the basic index for research on women. Each issue gives abstracts for over 200 articles and unannotated citations for several hundred more, selected from a wide variety of academic, professional, and feminist periodicals. Its arrangement begins with the tables of contents for recent numbers of women's studies journals and special issues of other periodicals, continues through 19 subject sections of interspersed abstracts and citations, and concludes with a section of 200-odd references to reviews of books on women. There are often book reviews and a bibliographic essay, as well. Quarterly indexes and annual cumulative index have varied in structure and scope over the years so that it is important to read the explanatory note at the beginning of each one.

013   Women's Work and Women's Studies, 1971-1973/74. New York: Barnard College Women's Center, 1972-75. 3 vols. (1971-72 distributed by KNOW, Inc., 1973/74 distributed by Feminist Press.)

An annual bibliography no longer published, this interdisciplinary tool lists completed works (including nonprint media), research in progress, and organizations in a subject arrangement whose headings reflect the bibliography's activist orientation. Although the citations to published research on any of the topics covered are now elsewhere available, these volumes as a group have no equal as a record of activity during four lively years of feminist scholarship.

See also: 033, 282.

Publications of One Type or Format

BIBLIOGRAPHIES AND REFERENCE BOOKS

014   EICHLER, MARGRIT. An Annotated Selected Bibliography of
       Bibliographies on Women. 2d rev. and enl. ed. Pittsburgh:
       KNOW, 1976. 33 pp.
           This compilation of ninety references was selected to
       include all major recent bibliographies that are readily
       accessible. Works cited are dated from the early twentieth
       century through the mid-seventies and include titles in
       several European languages, although the majority are from
       North America. (Canadian materials are especially well
       represented.) The annotations both describe each item's
       scope and evaluate its usefulness. Arrangement is alpha-
       betical by author with an index by broad subjects.

015   KOELLIKER, MARSHA DAVIS. A Bibliography of Bibliographies on
       Women Published since 1967. Master's research paper. Kent,
       Ohio: Kent State University School of Library Science,
       1973. 62 pp.
           The bibliographies listed are those published between
       January 1967 and December 1972 and cited in one of seven
       broad-spectrum indexes or catalogs, Bibliographic Index
       and National Union Catalog among them. Coverage is comp-
       rehensive: even footnotes and one-page reference lists
       are included, as are some foreign-language items. Highly
       technical topics are, however, excluded. Organization is
       by broad subject categories with author and title indexes.

016   McKEE, KATHLEEN BURKE. Women's Studies: A Guide to Reference
       Sources. Bibliography Series, no. 6. Storrs: University
       of Connecticut Library, 1977. 112 pp.
           Based on the collection of the University of Connecticut
       Library, this annotated bibliography of 364 items "is
       intended to be a guide to the new reference sources which
       deal with women's studies and also to reference sources from
       more traditional disciplines which are useful in women's

studies research." Citations are arranged by format:
Guides, Library catalogs. Handbooks, Directories, Statistics,
Indexes/abstracts/bibliographies. (This last section is
divided topically into more than thirty subsections.) Two
valuable features are a supplement listing women's serials
in the Library's Alternative Press Collection and the
inclusion, for any traditional reference work, of the
subject headings it uses for topics related to women.
There are author, title, and subject indexes.

017   SCHLACHTER, GAIL ANN and BELLI, DONNA. Minorities and Women:
      A Guide to Reference Sources in the Social Sciences. Los
      Angeles: Reference Service Press, 1977. 349 pp.
         Social science reference tools focusing on women are
      dispersed throughout this guide, since it is organized by
      format (fact books, biographical sources, documentary
      sources, directories, statistical sources, citation sources)
      with each format broken down into sections on minorities in
      general, specific minorities, and women. There are, for
      example, sixty-two citation sources--indexes, abstracts,
      bibliographies, and the like--given for women. Each title
      receives a lengthy descriptive annotation, and there are
      author, title, and subject indexes.

018   SECKELSON-SIMPSON, LINDA. With Reference to Women: An Annot-
      ated Bibliography of Reference Materials on Women in the
      Northwestern University Library. Evanston, Ill.: North-
      western University Library, 1975, addendum rev. May 1976.
      57 pp.
         This bibliography lists 175 books and serials, principally
      from the Northwestern University Library's Reference Depart-
      ment, that deal with women or with a particular subject
      associated with women, such as marriage, family planning,
      or divorce. The Library's extensive holdings in both older
      and recent materials, including a number in foreign lan-
      guages, and the length and quality of the annotations
      contribute to the value of this work. It is arranged by
      broad subject categories with an author/title/subject index.

019   WILLIAMSON, JANE. New Feminist Scholarship: A Guide to
      Bibliographies. Old Westbury, N.Y.: Feminist Press, 1979.
      139 pp.
         The 391 works cited in this book are English-language
      bibliographies, resource lists, and literature reviews
      published separately or as periodical articles, the majority
      since 1970. They are arranged in thirty subject categories,
      each prefaced by an explanatory note defining its scope and
      suggesting related sections. Some 52 percent of the entries
      have annotations, and there is a useful list of publishers'
      addresses as well as author and title indexes.

Bibliographies

INTERNATIONAL AND U.S. GOVERNMENT DOCUMENTS

020   AXEL-LUTE, PAUL. "Selected Federal Documents on Women's
       Rights." Women's Rights Law Reporter 4 (Winter 1978):
       126-32.
            U.S. government documents from 1963 through 1977 are
       listed chronologically within twenty topical divisions,
       with Superintendent of Documents classification number,
       brief annotation "where titles are not self-explanatory or
       where a work deserves special note," and (for congressional
       publications) the abstract number in CIS Index.

021   FERRISS, ABBOTT L. Indicators of Trends in the Status of
       American Women. New York: Russell Sage Foundation, 1971.
       451 pp.
            The book itself is a statistical rather than a biblio-
       graphical source, but since the data presented are derived
       primarily from U.S. government sources, the notes on sources
       together with the bibliography (pp. 433-51) form an effec-
       tive guide to federal documents providing statistical
       information on women.

*022   International Bibliography, Information, Documentation:
       Publications of International Organizations. Vol. 1-
       New York: Unipub, 1973- Quarterly.
            Each issue of this serial bibliography (also referred to
       by its acronym, IBID) lists and describes the generally
       available publications of several dozen international
       organizations which have been received during the previous
       quarter. One section of its broad subject classification
       is devoted to women, and the subject index contains further
       references to related titles in other sections.

*023   Women. Subject Bibliography SB-111. Washington: U.S. Govern-
       ment Printing Office. Annual? (revised regularly) This
       partially annotated, free price list comprises those U.S.
       government publications that were in print at the time of
       issue. The list dated June 5, 1978 cited nearly 200 titles,
       arranged alphabetically by title.

                                    See also: 098, 288, 294.

SPECIAL PERIODICAL ISSUES

024   CARDINALE, SUSAN. Special Issues of Serials about Women,
       1965-1975. Exchange Bibliography 995. Monticello, Ill.:
       Council of Planning Librarians, 1976. 41 pp.
            Special issues or sections from scholarly journals,
       popular magazines, and alternative press publications are
       listed alphabetically with descriptive annotations in this

bibliography. Issues on individual women are excluded.
The scope is nominally international but predominantly
North American.

025 EICHLER, MARGRIT; MARECKI, JOHN; and NEWTON, JENNIFER. <u>Women:</u>
<u>A Bibliography of Special Periodical Issues (1960-1975)</u>.
Canadian Newsletter of Research on Women, Special Publication no. 3. 1976. 75 pp.
  The 100-plus special issues or sections of periodicals
not normally devoted to the study of women listed here were
selected on the basis of their value for research. Most of
the titles included are of North American origin. Complete
tables of contents are reproduced for all but a handful
separately listed as an appendix. Continued by:

026 NEWTON, JENNIFER L. and ZAVITZ, CAROL. <u>Women: A Bibliography</u>
<u>of Special Periodical Issues</u>. Vol. 2. Canadian Newsletter
of Research on Women, Special Publication no. 4. 1978.
280 pp.
  This second volume adds roughly 375 special issues published from 1960 through 1977, with an addendum of issues
appearing before 1960. European coverage is much increased
--there are entries in eleven languages besides English and
French--and special indexes provide access to topics which
intersect a number of categories: Men, Family, Judaism and
Israeli studies, Immigration/Migration, Unions and Unioni-
zation, Agriculture and Rural Women. The concluding journal
index applies to both volumes 1 and 2.

*For continuing bibliographies which regularly note special periodi-
cal issues on women, <u>see</u> 006 and 012.

DISSERTATIONS

027 <u>Sex in Contemporary Society: A Catalog of Dissertations</u>.
Ann Arbor, Mich.: Xerox University Microfilms, 1973.
14 pp.
  There are citations but no abstracts in this list of
about 800 dissertations written between 1938 and 1973 and
available in microform or paper copy from University Microfilms. (No update is planned, but computer searches can
be arranged.) Titles are listed within fifteen subject
categories, principally from the social sciences but also
including religion, literature, cinema, and (despite the
catalog's title) history.

See also: 334.

WOMEN'S MOVEMENT PUBLICATIONS

Bibliographic resources described in this section are concerned with
the contemporary women's movement and not with historic feminism.

028   JOAN, POLLY and CHESMAN, ANDREA. <u>Guide to Women's Publishing</u>.
       Paradise, Calif.: Dustbooks, 1978. 296 pp.
          The major chapters in this directory are concerned with
       feminist journals, women's newspapers (including news
       services), women's presses (including print shops), and
       distributors. Address, frequency, price, and often format
       of publications are given, as well as a description of
       editorial policy and types of material published. A final
       chapter lists such additional resources as directories,
       review publications, support organizations, and bookstores.

*029   <u>Media Report to Women Index/Directory</u>. Washington: Women's
       Institute for Freedom of the Press, 1972- Annual.
          This publication combines the annual index for the
       monthly <u>Media Report to Women</u> with a directory of women's
       media. Among the seventeen types of media listed and
       briefly described in the 1977 Directory were periodicals,
       library collections, and directories or catalogs. Entries
       are compiled from questionnaires sent out each year, making
       the list of periodicals the best updated of those available.

030   <u>The New Woman's Survival Sourcebook</u>. Ed. Kirsten Grimstad and
       Susan Rennie. New York: Knopf, 1975. 245 pp.
          This feminist catalog describes organizations, services,
       and publications in the U.S., Canada, and England created
       by women "for the control of their own lives." The topical
       chapters, most of which have subdivisions, are made up of
       one or more essays, followed by descriptions of resources
       relevant to the topic such as women's bookstores, publishers,
       newspapers, periodicals, books, and pamphlets. Full order
       information is given for all publications, and an author/
       title index makes it possible to locate specific items.
       Continued by:

031   GRIMSTAD, KIRSTEN, et al. "Feminist Publishing." Parts 1-2.
       <u>Chrysalis</u>, no. 2 (1977), pp. 101-111; no. 3 (1977), pp.
       79-91.
          The history and special interests of most of the pub-
       lishers represented in this catalog are stated, and there
       is an extensive annotation for each title they list. The
       editors of <u>Chrysalis</u> have announced that feminist publishing
       will be one of their regular features.

See also: 016.

LIBRARY CATALOGS

032   ARTHUR and ELIZABETH SCHLESINGER LIBRARY ON THE HISTORY OF
      WOMEN IN AMERICA. The Manuscript Inventories and the
      Catalogs of Manuscripts, Books, and Pictures. Boston:
      G.K. Hall, 1973. 3 vols.
          This photographically reproduced catalog of "probably
      the largest collection of source material on the history
      of women in America, except for the Library of Congress,"
      reflects especially strong holdings in suffrage, social
      reform, and women in the professions and labor movement.
      Contents: vols. 1-2: Dictionary catalog of the book col-
      lection, including main entry cards for books on women in
      Harvard's Widener Library, and separate listings for the
      etiquette and periodical collections; vol. 3: Manuscript
      catalog, manuscript inventories (describing individual
      collections), and picture catalog. An update covering
      acquisitions since 1973 is planned.

*033 BiblioFem: The Joint Library Catalogues of the Fawcett Library
      and the Equal Opportunities Commission Together with a
      Continuing Bibliography on Women. London: Fawcett Library,
      City of London Polytechnic, 1978- Monthly. Microfiche (42x).
          The Fawcett Library is the principal British historical
      collection on women, especially women's rights; the EOC
      Information Centre collects contemporary materials on women's
      rights and equal opportunity. This computer-produced micro-
      fiche catalog represents not only their combined current
      acquisitions but, more importantly, all publications on
      women being catalogued by either Library of Congress or the
      British Library and available as MARC records. These titles
      are being added to BiblioFem both as they are cataloged and
      retrospectively, so that in early 1979 the catalog was
      complete for 1977 and 1978, with 1979 and 1976 due to be
      added next. Each monthly issue contains two versions of
      the entire catalog to date: an alphabetical author/title/
      series catalog, and a classed catalog based on a modified
      Dewey Decimal Classification.

034   INDIANA. University. Institute for Sex Research. Library.
      Catalog of the Social and Behavioral Sciences. Monograph
      Section. Boston: G.K. Hall, 1974. 4 vols.

035   _____. Catalog of Periodical Literature in the Social and
      Behavioral Sciences Section...Including Supplement to
      Monographs 1973-1975. Boston: G.K. Hall, 1976. 4 vols.
          The monographs catalog consists of "historical materials
      relating to sex behavior, including histories of early sex
      education, marriage, abortion, contraception, women's rights,

sex ethics, religion, sex laws, venereal disease and pros-
titution, as well as contemporary research in sex behavior
and attitudes." Printed works of all languages and periods
are represented but Western nineteenth and twentieth century
materials predominate. The Institute's collection of erotic
art and literature is not included but bibliographies on
the subject and censorship studies are. The periodicals
catalog indexes journals received in the library and reprints located through a widely interdisciplinary literature
search conducted between October 1973 and November 1975,
plus 10,000 others received earlier but not indexed.

036 INTERNATIONAAL ARCHIEF VOOR DE VROUWENBEWEGING, AMSTERDAM.
Catalogue of the Library of the International Archives
for the Women's Movement. Boston: G. K. Hall, forthcoming.
3 vols.
Founded in 1935 to preserve the documents of pioneer
feminists and to establish a book collection for the study
of women, the archives have continued to serve the dual
purpose of collecting manuscript and printed materials on
the women's movement worldwide. The publishers announce
that this reproduction of the card catalog in book form
will provide both author and subject access.

037 NORTH CAROLINA. University at Greensboro. Library. The
Woman's Collection at the University of North Carolina at
Greensboro: A Checklist of Holdings. Comp. Marda Scott
and Elizabeth Power. Greensboro: Walter Clinton Jackson
Library, 1975. 150 pp.
The works of major feminists and North Carolina
women are featured in this author catalog of a collection
of about 2,000 European and American books by and about
women. Writings in English, French, and German are included. Most were published from the seventeenth through
the nineteenth centuries, with some titles dating from the
first half of the twentieth century.

038 SOPHIA SMITH COLLECTION. Catalogs of the Sophia Smith Collection, Women's History Archive, Smith College, Northampton,
Massachusetts. Boston: G. K. Hall, 1975. 7 vols.
This catalog reflects an outstanding collection of books
and manuscripts on women, not restricted to women in the
U.S., although it emphasizes the history of American women.
Topics covered represent both the humanities and the social
sciences and extend in time from the eighteenth century to
the present day. Contents: vols. 1-2: Author catalog
(including articles from periodicals in the collection);
vols. 3-5: Subject catalog; vols. 6-7: Manuscript and
photograph catalogs.

See also: 069.

Bibliographies

GUIDES TO ARCHIVES AND MANUSCRIPT COLLECTIONS

United States

For state repositories such as historical societies, some of
which have extensive holdings not limited in subject to that
state, <u>see</u>: 057, 058, 065, 066, 070.

039 U.S. LIBRARY OF CONGRESS. Manuscript Division. <u>The Blackwell
Family, Carrie Chapman Catt, and the National Woman Suffrage Association: A Register of Their Papers in the
Library of Congress</u>. Washington: U.S. Govt. Print. Off.
1975. 102 pp.

040 WILSON, JOAN HOFF and DONOVAN, LYNN BONFIELD. "Women's
History: A Listing of West Coast Archival and Manuscript
Sources." Parts 1-2. <u>California Historical Quarterly</u> 55,
no. 1 (Spring 1976): 74-83; no. 2 (Summer 1976): 170-85.
 Together the two parts describe collections in forty-
one repositories (32 in California, 2 in Oregon, 5 in
Washington, 2 in British Columbia). The degree of detail
submitted by the institutions varies, but in most cases
they provide the names of individual women whose papers
they hold and the amount of material represented.

041 <u>Women's History Sources: A Guide to Archives and Manuscript
Collections in the United States</u>. Ed. Andrea Hinding.
New York: Bowker, forthcoming. 2 vols.
 The publisher announces that "this massive work describes
more than 18,000 collections in 1,600 repositories, nation-
wide, documenting the lives of American women from Colonial
times to the present. . . . Included for each entry: collection title, physical description (type of documents,
inclusive dates, etc.), information about access to collections and bibliographic control (guide, card catalog,
project description, etc.), repository title, and a concise
description of collection contents."

See also: 143, 244, 293, 295.

Canada

042 RIELLY, HEATHER, and HINDMARCH, MARILYN. <u>Some Sources for
Women's History in the Public Archives of Canada</u>. National
Museum of Man Mercury Series, History Division Paper no. 5.
Ottawa: National Museums of Canada, 1974. 93 pp.
 This guide to selected English-language private papers
in the Public Archives describes entire collections of
the papers of individual women or women's organizations
and those portions of other collections that are concerned
with women.

See also: 006, 080, 084, 088.

Great Britain

043 LIPSHITZ, SUSAN. Sexual Politics in Britain: A Bibliographical Guide with Historical Notes. . .Companion to the
Sexual Politics in Britain Collection. Hassocks, Sussex:
Harvester Press, 1977. 41 pp.
    The text of this guide describes twelve British feminist
groups, chiefly radical and/or lesbian, whose papers make
up a commercially issued microfiche collection.

044 WEEKS, JEFFREY. "Notes on Sources: The Women's Movement."
Bulletin of the Society for the Study of Labour History no.
29 (Autumn 1974):55-59.
    This bibliographic essay on the principal archives and
manuscript repositories useful for research in the history
of the British women's movement from about 1870 to 1914
includes social morality campaigns, suffrage, pressure
groups, working class women, maternity and child welfare,
and family planning.

Australia

045 Women in Australia: An Annotated Guide to Records. Ed. Kay
Daniels, Mary Murnane, and Ann Picot. Canberra: Australian
Government Publishing Service, 1977. 2 vols.
    This guide to archival and manuscript collections of
state archives, libraries and other institutions, and
individuals is geographically arranged with a subject index.
Since the compilers "have chosen to expand the concept of
records relating to women to take in the sources that reveal
the experiences of women in society" and have provided
extensive annotations, in some cases amounting to short
essays, the work itself contains a quantity of Australian
social history. In addition, there are useful lists of
finding aids (indexes, bibliographies, guides) and collective biographies on women in Australia and on the country
in general.

046 Women in Australian Society, 1901-45: A Guide to Holdings of
Australian Archives Relating to Women, 1901-45. Ed. Janet
Reed and Kathleen Oakes. Canberra: Australian Government
Publishing Service, 1977. 121 pp.
    Restricted to the holdings of the three main branches
of the Australian federal archives and not duplicating the
title above, this work provides brief descriptions of groups
of records directly concerned with women. It is organized
by subject, with chapters on women's traditional role, work,
health, education, law, politics, aboriginal women, migrant
women, women in the External Territories, and a few
individuals.

BIOGRAPHIES/AUTOBIOGRAPHIES/DIARIES

047 BEGOS, JANE DUPREE. Annotated Bibliography of Published
Women's Diaries. Pound Ridge, N.Y.: the author, 1977.
66 pp. Available from Jane Begos, Eastwoods Rd., Pound
Ridge, N.Y. 10576.
This is a compilation of brief annotations for over 500
"actual diaries, works that call themselves diaries and
aren't; works that don't call themselves diaries and are;
and works that are based on actual diaries or written in
diary form." Although nearly all of them are in English,
their authors represent a number of European and Asian
countries as well as Great Britain and North America. They
vary in period from the seventeenth century's Lady Margaret
Hoby to persons still living.

048 GROS-LOUIS, DOLORES K. Autobiographies of American Women: An
Annotated Bibliography. Bloomington: Indiana University
Press, forthcoming.
The compiler informs me that the work will include published autobiographies (excluding oral histories and short
autobiographies in periodicals) and manuscript autobiographies of twenty pages or more, especially those in major
archives.

049 IRELAND, NORMA OLIN. Index to Women of the World from Ancient
to Modern Times: Biographies and Portraits. Westwood,
Mass.: Faxon, 1970. 573 pp.
Approximately 13,000 women are included in this index to
articles in 945 collective biographies. With minor excep-
tions the works analyzed are from the early twentieth
century through 1968. Since dates, nationality, and occupation are given for the women listed, this book can be
used by itself to identify a woman for whom only the name
is known.

050 RHODES, CAROLYN H. First Person Female American: A Selected
and Annotated Bibliography of the Autobiographies of American Women Living after 1950. Troy, N.Y.: Whitston Publishing Co., forthcoming.
This was originally announced as a supplement to the
September 1977 issue of American Notes and Queries.

See also: 062, 143.

ORAL HISTORY

051 BORNAT, JOANNA. "Women's History and Oral History: An Outline
Bibliography." Oral History 5 (Autumn 1977):124-35.

This bibliographic essay identifies examples of the antecedents of women's oral history (social investigation, anthropological research, autobiography), recent writings using oral history of women as a source, and some uses of interview material by nonprint media.

052 "Selected Bibliography and Resources In Women's Oral History." *Frontiers* 2 (Summer 1977):122-24.
This bibliography of recent materials, chiefly since 1970, is arranged by format: bibliographies/guides/manuals; directories; journals/newsletters; works on methods; published oral histories; nonprint media.

Geographical Subjects

This section lists all bibliographies limited to materials on women
within one geographical area or political unit except for those
concerned with: (1) Guides to archives and manuscript collections;
(2) History of the U.S., Canada, Great Britain, and Europe; (3) National literatures; and (4) Topical subjects in the context of U.S. society
or culture.   Consult the Table of Contents to locate the sections for
these subjects.

UNITED STATES--GENERAL AND REGIONAL

053   FARR, SIDNEY SAYLOR.   Appalachian Women, 1830-1979:   A Biblio-
      ography.   Lexington: University Press of Kentucky, forth-
      coming.
          According to the compiler, this is a compilation of about
      1,200 entries, most of them annotated, divided into fourteen
      subject categories.   Books, chapters from books, and articles
      from a variety of periodicals are included.

054   HABER, BARBARA.   Women in America: A Guide to Books, 1963-
      1975.   Boston: G.K. Hall, 1978.   202 pp.
          This annotated bibliography seeks to document the new
      feminism (since The Feminine Mystique) by identifying out-
      standing books that might serve as a library core collec-
      tion on women's studies or as readings for women's studies
      courses, undergraduates, or general readers.   Belles-lettres,
      children's books, technical works, reference books, and
      reprints are excluded.   The organization of the eighteen
      subject chapters follows the issues the books discuss, from
      "Abortion" through "Work."   Several titles within each
      category have essay-length annotations; other annotations
      are briefer but still evaluative.   There is an author/title
      index.

055   PATTERSON-BLACK, SHERYL and PATTERSON-BLACK, GENE. <u>Western</u>
      <u>Women in History and Literature</u>. Crawford, Neb.: Cotton-
      wood Press, 1978. [unpaginated] Available from Cottonwood
      Press, P.O. Drawer 112, Crawford, NB 69339.
         The more than 2,000 titles listed in this briefly annot-
      ated bibliography comprise "materials by and about women in
      the American West from pre-Anglo settlement through World
      War II," with concentration primarily on the continental
      U.S. west of the Missouri-Mississippi Rivers but also in-
      cluding some items on Alaska, Hawaii, and western Canada.
      Arrangement is by literary form: Essays on Women's Work in
      the Frontier West and on Women Homesteaders on the Great
      Plains, Research Tools and General Background Studies, Oral
      History/Biography, Letters/Diaries/Autobiographical Writings,
      Literature. Several of the sections include manuscript
      materials as well as published writings.

056   "Women In The South: A Bibliography." <u>Southern Exposure</u> 4
      (Winter 1977):98-103.
         Books, articles, and a few unpublished dissertations are
      listed in this bibliography of over 150 items. They are
      organized in broad categories: Theory; General (cultural,
      historical, and sociological studies); Autobiographies/
      Biographies/Memoirs; Literature.

UNITED STATES--SPECIFIC STATES

   <u>Alaska</u>

   <u>See</u> 074.

   <u>Georgia</u>

057   <u>Women's Records: A Preliminary Guide</u>. Comp. Darlene R. Roth
      and Virginia Shadron. Atlanta: Georgia Dept. of Archives
      and History, 1978. 70 pp.
         Only the Manuscripts Section of the Georgia Archives and
      not the more extensive Government Records Office is covered
      by this guide. It provides succinct descriptions of 142
      collections listed alphabetically within 3 groups: individ-
      uals, families, organizations. The introduction states that
      these listings are more complete than those submitted to
      <u>Women's History Sources</u>.

Illinois

058 BECK, NELSON. <u>Resources for the Study of Women's History
     Located in the Illinois Historical Survey Library</u>. Urbana:
     Illinois Historical Survey Library, 1979. 9 pp.

Maine

059 LITOFF, JUDY BARRETT and LITOFF, HAL. "Working Women in Maine:
     A Note on Sources." <u>Labor History</u> 17 (Winter 1976):88-95.
          This review essay identifies some thirty published and
     unpublished sources from colonial times to the present day,
     including books, articles, theses, state documents, archival
     collections, and newspaper files.

060 OSTROFF, SUSAN. "Selected Bibliography" in <u>A Woman's Place
     . . .The Maine Point of View</u>. Augusta: Maine State Museum,
     1977, pp. 33-44.
          Part of the catalog for a Bicentennial exhibition, this
     annotated bibliography cites ninety-one publications in
     categories that include primary and secondary sources,
     belles-lettres, and juvenile literature, as well as de-
     scribing manuscript collections on women in four Maine
     repositories.

Michigan

061 <u>Bibliography of Sources Relating to Women</u>. Lansing: Michigan
     History Division, Michigan Dept. of State, 1975. 27 pp.
     Available from EDRS, ED 128 683.
          The State Archives and six other manuscript repositories
     chose the collections they felt were potentially most useful
     for research on women to be described in this cooperative
     finding aid. The materials represented include personal
     papers, the records of women's organizations, and archival
     collections of government agencies concerned with women.

062 <u>Michigan Women: Biographies, Autobiographies, and Reminis-
     cences</u>. Lansing: State Library Services, Michigan Dept.
     of Education, 1975. 7 pp.
          About 100 titles from the Michigan Collection in the
     State Library are arranged alphabetically by the name of
     the woman who is the subject of the book.

Minnesota

063 PALMQUIST, BONNIE BEATSON. "Women in Minnesota History,
     1915-1976: An Annotated Bibliography of Articles Pertaining
     to Women." <u>Minnesota History</u> 45 (1977):187-91.

New Jersey

064   STEINER-SCOTT, ELIZABETH and WAGLE, ELIZABETH PEARCE. <u>New
      Jersey Women, 1770-1970: A Bibliography</u>. Rutherford,
      N.J.: Fairleigh Dickinson University Press, 1978. 167 pp.
          This bibliography lists separately published materials
      and periodical articles dealing with women's role in the
      state's history, their social and economic conditions, and
      general attitudes towards women. The 1,340 entries are
      divided into 24 chapters covering historical periods,
      topical subjects, and literary genres, and there is an
      author/subject index.

North Carolina

065   THOMPSON, CATHERINE E. <u>A Selective Guide to Women-related
      Records in the North Carolina State Archives</u>. Raleigh:
      North Carolina Division of Archives and History, 1977.
      77 pp.

                                              See also: 037.

Ohio

066   WESTERN RESERVE HISTORICAL SOCIETY, CLEVELAND. Genealogical
      Committee. <u>Index to the Microfilm Edition of Genealogical
      Data Relating to Women in the Western Reserve before 1840
      (1850)</u>. Cleveland, Ohio: The Committee, 1976. 226 pp.

South Dakota

067   SOUTH DAKOTA COMMISSION ON THE STATUS OF WOMEN. <u>South Dakota
      Women, 1850-1919: A Bibliography</u>. Pierre: The Commission,
      1975. 23 pp.
          "This bibliography includes books and pamphlets on South
      Dakota women from 1850 settlements through 1919 ratification
      of the suffrage amendment." County histories and periodi-
      cals are excluded; juvenile literature is not. For each
      entry there is a descriptive annotation and a symbol lo-
      cating at least one copy in a library within the state.

Vermont

068   PEPE, FAITH L. "Toward a History of Women in Vermont: An
      Essay and Bibliography." <u>Vermont History</u> 45 (Spring
      1977):69-101.

The review essay discusses sources for the study of
Vermont women and cites about thirty-five titles in its
notes. The bibliography lists over 200 items, including
both published and manuscript materials, in a detailed
subject arrangement.

Virginia

069   LIPSCOMB LIBRARY. The Collection of Writings by Virginia
      Women in the Lipscomb Library, Randolph-Macon Woman's
      College: A Catalog of the Collection. Lynchburg, Va.:
      Alumnae Association of Randolph-Macon Woman's College,
      1974. 98 pp.
           This is an author listing of works written, edited, or
      compiled by women born in Virginia or identified with the
      state through long residence.

Wisconsin

070   DANKY, JAMES P. and McKAY, ELEANOR. Women's History: Re-
      sources at the State Historical Society of Wisconsin. 3d
      ed. enl. Madison: State Historical Society of Wisconsin,
      1976. 29 pp.
           This guide to the Society's collections of published
      materials, archives and manuscripts, photographs, and
      artifacts for research in women's history includes some
      information on related collections at the University of
      Wisconsin-Madison. Although it is the principal repository
      for the papers of Wisconsin individuals and organizations,
      the Society's holdings are far from being confined to
      Wisconsin materials and are especially rich in labor history
      and social activism.

CANADA--GENERAL AND REGIONAL

071   BRACHER, MICHAEL D. and KRISHNAN, P.   "Family and Demography:
      A Selected Canadian Bibliography." Journal of Comparative
      Family Studies 7 (Summer 1976):367-72.
           This alphabetical listing of approximately eighty
      references from 1967 through 1975 includes scholarly books,
      articles, and conference papers in English and (occasionally)
      French.

072   EICHLER, MARGRIT. "Review Essay: Sociology of Feminist
      Research in Canada." Signs 3 (Winter 1977):409-22.

This survey of feminist social research since 1970 is organized by the main issues involved: cultural, economic, legal, physiological, and psychic dependency, isolation within the nuclear family, and the double dependency of female members of marginal groups. About 100 books, articles, theses, and conference papers are listed in the footnotes.

073 _____. "Sociological Research on Women in Canada." Canadian Review of Sociology and Anthropology/Revue canadienne de Sociologie et d'Anthropologie 12 (Nov. 1975):474-81.
      The author names examples of noteworthy publications, pointing out the emphasis given research on working women, especially professional women, and identifying gaps in the sociological literature. The reference list of eighty-eight books and articles consists chiefly of titles published from 1965 through 1974.

074 "La Femme Et Le Nord . . . Women And The North: A Bibliography Of Biographies, Autobiographies, Journals And Fiction Written By, Or Written About, Women In The Canadian North And Alaska." North 22 (Oct. 1975):62-63.
      Most of the eight French and forty-nine English works listed in this bilingual bibliography have annotations in the language of the title. Publication dates range from 1903 to 1975, and both Native American and European women are represented.

075 GERMAIN SAMSON, MARCELLE. Des livres et des femmes: Bibliographie. Québec: Conseil du statut de la femme, Gouvernement du Québec, 1978. 254 pp.
      Since it is intended for francophone women, nearly all the titles in this partially annotated bibliography of 1,357 entries are in French, even to French translations of Margaret Mead and Betty Friedan. For such readers, the work is useful as an interdisciplinary general bibliography focused on Quebec and Canadian authors, mainly for the period 1940-1978. For English-speaking scholars with a command of French, the value of the book lies in the sections on feminism and women's history in Canada and in France, especially some 500 titles derived from the holdings of the Bibliothèque Marguerite Durand in Paris. In addition to these sections, topical divisions cover society and politics, law, work, education, sexuality, marriage and family, aggression, and (more briefly) fiction and humor. There is an author index.

076 HAUCK, PHILOMENA. Sourcebook on Canadian Women. Ottawa: Canadian Library Association, 1979. 111 pp.

This inclusive guide to currently available English-language materials lists books, periodicals, pamphlets, audiovisual materials, and general information sources in catalog format. Entries are arranged in subject chapters: Women's Rights; Law, Work, and Day Care; Health; Biography; Literature; Children's Books; Periodicals; Audiovisual Materials; General Bibliographies and Information Sources. The book concludes with a list of publishers and an author/ title index.

077   MAZUR, CAROL and PEPPER, SHEILA. Women in Canada, 1965 to 1975: A Bibliography. Hamilton, Ont.: McMaster University Library Press, 1976. 174 pp.
      This is the most comprehensive bibliography on contemporary Canadian women. Under nearly 300 subject headings the compilers list 1,973 citations to books, theses, journal and newspaper articles, and government documents in English and French. (This number includes some repetition of titles falling into more than one category.) Since headings are arranged alphabetically rather than topically, it is essential to consult the table of contents to discover all the headings relevant to any subject. Author index.

078   SWANICK, M. LYNNE STRUTHERS. Women in Canadian Politics and Government: A Bibliography. Exchange Bibliography 697. Monticello, Ill.: Council of Planning Librarians, 1974. 29 pp.
      This bibliography lists 245 books, articles, and documents on the rights and political participation of Canadian women in alphabetical sequence with a subject index. It also includes lists of government bodies concerned with women and women's magazines distributed nationally.

079   WILSON, MARION C. Women in Federal Politics: A Bio-bibliography. Ottawa: National Library of Canada, 1975. 81 pp.
      For each of the members of Parliament and senators since 1920, this bilingual work gives a brief biography, a list of sources, and a selected list of publications. There is also a brief general bibliography (fifty-one items) on women in federal politics.

CANADA--SPECIFIC PROVINCES

Alberta

080   SILVERMAN, ELIANE LESLAU and MUIR, RODNEY ANNE. "Archival Holdings in Canadian Women's History: Alberta, Manitoba, and Saskatchewan." Canadian Newsletter of Research on Women 6 (Feb. 1977):127-30.

Manitoba

081 Out from the Shadows: A Bibliography of the History of Women
in Manitoba. Researched and compiled by Pam Atnikov et al.
Winnipeg: Manitoba Human Rights Commission, 1975. 64 pp.
This selected bibliography aims at sampling many areas
rather than comprehensive coverage. Briefly annotated
citations to about 450 books, chapters from books, and
periodical articles, all in English and available in
Winnipeg, are arranged in subject categories: law, politics,
employment, and society/culture. The final section lists
bibliographies.

082 SMITH, MARILYN. Women in Manitoba History: Herstory, Re-
search, and Bibliography. Winnipeg: Historic Resources
Branch, Manitoba Dept. of Tourism, Recreation, and Cultural
Affairs, 1974. [unpaginated.]

See also: 080.

Ontario

083 ACTION, JANICE; GOLDSMITH, PENNY; and SHEPHERD, BONNIE. "Bibliography" in Women at Work: Ontario, 1850-1930. Toronto:
Canadian Women's Educational Press, 1974, pp. 369-405.

084 LIGHT, BETH. "An Inventory of Sources on Women in the Personal
Papers, Family Papers and Manuscript Collection in the
Archives of Ontario." Canadian Newsletter of Research on
Women 6 (Supp. Feb. 1977):171-95.

Québec

085 HOULE, GHISLAINE. La Femme et la societé québécoise. Bibliographies québécoises, no. 1. Montreal: Bibliothèque
Nationale du Québec, Ministère des affaires culturelles,
1975. 228 pp.
This partially annotated bibliography of 1,400 books,
government documents, and periodical articles includes
materials in both French and English, although headings and
introductory matter are in French only. Its organization
is by broad subjects (political rights and legal status,
work, sexuality, advancement, general works, literature,
biographies), concluding with lists of women's periodicals
and organizations. There are author and title indexes.

086 MARANDA, JEANNE and VERTHUY, MAIR. "Québec Feminist Writing."
Emergency Librarian 5 (Sept.-Oct. 1977):3-11.

A sruvey article and chronology for the years 1971-1977 are accompanied by an annotated bibliography arranged by year and genre: literary works, manifestoes, periodical publications, studies/surveys. A French translation of the article and bibliography follows on pages 12-20.

087 QUÉBEC (Province). Conseil du statut de la femme. Les Québec-oises: Guide bibliographique suivi d'une filmographie. Collection "Etudes et dossiers." Québec: Editeur officiel du Québec, 1976. 160 pp.

088 SOCIÉTÉ HISTORIQUE DU CANADA. Comité de l'histoire des femmes. "Rapport sur les archives au Québec." Canadian Newsletter of Research on Women 5 (Oct. 1976):87-89.

A classified list of Québec archives useful for research in the history of women is arranged by type of collection (universities, women's organizations, personal papers, newspapers, libraries, and national, regional, religious, audiovisual, trade union, and educational associations), with individual collections in each group identified.

Saskatchewan

See: 080.

EUROPE AND EUROPEAN COUNTRIES

089 DUNN, SEPHEN P. and DUNN, ETHEL. The Study of the Soviet Family in the USSR and in the West. Slavic Studies Working Paper no. 1. Columbus, Ohio: American Association for the Advancement of Slavic Studies, 1977. 75 pp.

This paper seeks "to make a selective inventory of what is available on the Soviet family in Russian and in English for various historical periods, to note gaps and discrepancies, and to point out a few of the major characteristics discernible in recent Soviet and Western treatments of the subject." The 184 notes, some containing a dozen or more titles, constitute a valuable if unwieldy listing of studies on the family among Russian and non-Russian Soviet peoples.

090 GOLD, CAROL. "Women in Scandinavia: A Bibliography of Material in English." Scandinavian Review 65 (Sept. 1977):83-85.

This bibliography of eighty-six items lists materials dated from as early as 1856 through 1977. Books, government documents, and journal articles are organized under subject categories which include sex roles and family, employment, law, politics, literature, and feminism.

091 VREEDE DE STUERS, CORA. "Women Migrants in Western Europe."
     Canadian Newsletter of Research on Women 7 (July 1978):90-94.
        Condensed from a more extensive work annotated in Dutch,
     this review article outlines the chief points of women
     migrants' position in Europe and summarizes the state of
     research on the topic. The selected bibliography of thirty-
     eight items in English, French, German, and Dutch is coded
     by nationality of migrants and by main topic, such as
     housing or working conditions.

                                            See also: 075, 105.

THIRD WORLD

092 BIRDSALL, NANCY. An Introduction to the Social Science Litera-
     ture on "Women's Place" and Fertility in the Developing
     World. Annotated Bibliography, vol. 2, no. 1. Washington:
     Interdisciplinary Communicatons Program, Smithsonian
     Institution, 1974. 39 pp.
        A bibliographic essay on the relationship between the
     status of women and fertility rates in developing countries
     introduces about 100 abstracts of recently published and
     unpublished sources, alphabetically ordered with a geograph-
     ical index. A list of addresses for journals, organizations,
     and publishers is appended.

093 BUVINIĆ, MAYRA. Women and World Development: An Annotated
     Bibliography. Prepared under the auspices of the American
     Association for the Advancement of Science. Washington:
     Overseas Development Council, 1976. 162 pp. Also published
     in AAAS Seminar on Women in Development, Mexico, 1975.
     Women and World Development. New York: Praeger, 1976.
        This work selects and abstracts 381 books, articles,
     dissertations, and conference papers, focusing on "the
     effects of socio-economic development and cultural change
     on women and on women's reactions to these changes." Most
     of the materials are in English and have been published
     since 1970. They are organized in topical sections sub-
     divided by broad geographical area. An introductory essay
     offers "A Critical Review of Some Research Concepts and
     Concerns." Lists of special journals and of bibliographies
     related to women and development conclude the volume.

094 Non-formal Education and the Role of Women and Families in
     Human Resource Development. Topical Acquisitions List no.
     4. East Lansing: Non-formal Education Information Center,
     Institute for International Studies in Education, Michigan
     State University, 1976. 29 pp. Available from EDRS, ED
     132 353.
        This list of writings concerned with women in development
     and with nonformal education programs directed primarily

towards women and families includes sections on topics
such as family planning, health, nutrition, home economics,
literacy, agriculture, and teacher/leadership training. A
large proportion of the 238 references are government
documents, conference reports, pamphlets, or unpublished
papers, and there is an appended list of 23 conferences
seminars on women and development.

095   RIHANI, MAY. Development as if Women Mattered: An Annotated
Bibliography with a Third World Focus. Occasional Paper
no. 10. Washington: Secretariat for Women in Development,
New TransCentury Foundation, 1978. 137 pp.
   Concern over the effect that the programs of development
agencies were having upon women in their target areas
prompted the compilation of this bibliography of 287 evaluative abstracts. Its aim is to supplement existing bibliographies by focusing on action-oriented publications,
those written from a Third World viewpoint, and unpublished
papers available in photocopy from the Foundation. Organization is by subject categories subdivided geographically,
with cross references to related material in other sections.
The introduction summarizes important findings and recom-
mendations of the writings included. A list of other
bibliographies and an author index conclude the work.

096   SAULNIERS, SUZANNE SMITH and RAKOWSKI, CATHY A. Women in the
Development Process: A Select Bibliography on Women in
Sub-Saharan Africa and Latin America. Austin: Institute
of Latin American Studies, University of Texas, 1977.
287 pp.
   Emphasis is on sociological and anthropological writings
in this bibliography of books, articles, conference papers,
pamphlets, and unpublished documents, in general dated from
1900 through 1976. Because the African and Latin American
sections were separately compiled, their scope varies some-
what. The African compiler covered the period 1900-1975,
noting the scarcity of materials on women in South Africa
and making little effort to cover labor legislation and
legal status of women. The Latin American compiler concen-
trated on titles published after 1930, especially those
most recent, and included more material on revolutionary
women and feminism. Both sections exclude fertility and
family planning as a topic, although literature on the
Latin American family is included. The 2,844 citations are
arranged in broad subject divisions, each subdivided by
topic and, within topic, by geographic area, so that it is
easy to locate materials on specific subjects. There are
also three supplementary bibliographies of general references, sources consulted, and periodicals cited.

097   "Selected Bibliography On Women." <u>NFE Exchange</u>, no. 13
       (1978): pp. 10-18. Available from Non-formal Education
       Information Center, Institute for International Studies in
       Education, Michigan State University.
          This list of holdings of the NFE Library concerned with
       women and world development contains more than seventy
       annotations for books, pamphlets, reports, and international
       documents, none earlier than 1970, as well as lists of
       journals, newsletters, and special issues. <u>NFE Exchange</u>
       regularly includes reports of publications on women and
       development.

098   <u>Women and Family in Rural Development: Annotated Bibliography</u>.
       n.p.: Documentation Centre and Population Documentation
       Centre, Food and Agriculture Organization of the United
       Nations, 1977. 58 pp.
          This index to FAO publications from 1966 to mid-1976
       was produced by a search based on the descriptors Women,
       Family, Home, and some related terms. Citations are listed
       chronologically with author and keyword indexes. The
       synopsis of each document is in English; the papers them-
       selves are in more than thirty languages, with English the
       most common.

099   <u>Women in Development: A Bibliography</u>. 3d ed. The Hague:
       Institute of Social Studies, 1978. 56 pp.
          The preface describes this as a revised and updated
       version of a bibliography compiled by Marco Bloemendaal.
       It lists publications on Third World women added to the
       ISS collection through the academic year 1977-78. Both
       current and older writings are included, but no systematic
       search was made of periodical literature before 1975. The
       sizable portion of the entries originating in Europe or the
       Third World gives the bibliography its chief value; nonethe-
       less, all but a handful of the 549 references are in English,
       with no indication that any are translations. They are
       organized into ten topical divisions, plus sections for
       general works and bibliographies and a final section pro-
       viding annotations for 100 of the previous entries. Since
       there are no indexes, there is no way of locating material
       on women in a particular country or area.

100   "Women In Rural Development." <u>Rural Development Network Bul-</u>
       <u>letin</u>, no. 6, pt. 1 (July 1976), pp. 1-20; no. 6, pt. 2
       (May 1977), pp. 1-25. Available from Overseas Liaison Com-
       mittee, American Council on Education, 11 Dupont Circle, NW,
       Washington, D.C. 20036.
          Part 1 summarizes "current research and action programs;
       conferences and workshops; publications and films focusing

on rural women in developing countries of Africa and Latin America--and to some extent Asia and the Caribbean." Part 2 adds further references of the same sort, including some for the Middle East.

See also: 526.

LATIN AMERICA

101   CARLOS, MANUEL L. and SELLERS, LOIS. "Family, Kinship Struc-
       ture and Modernization in Latin America." Latin American
       Research Review 7 (Summer 1972):95-124.
            An analysis of "family and kinship patterns in Latin
       America among distinct socio-economic groups in urban and
       rural settings" is followed by a critical examination of
       the literature on which the analysis is based. All of the
       100-plus references are in English and most were published
       after 1960.

102   KINZER, NORA SCOTT. "Priests, Machos, and Babies; or, Latin
       American Women and the Manichaean Heresy." Journal of
       Marriage and the Family 35 (May 1973):300-312.
            A review of recent sociological research and popular
       literature indicates that the influence of the Roman Catholic
       Church and the importance of machismo are generally assigned
       too great responsibility for Latin America's high birth rate
       and that female unemployment and illiteracy are of more
       significance. The list of references cites 218 titles.

103.   KNASTER, MERI. "Women in Latin America: The State of Re-
       search, 1975." Latin American Research Review 11, no. 1
       (1976):3-74.
            This review of research activities concerned with women
       in Latin America emphasizes material published from 1970
       through 1975, updating and expanding the material in
       Pescatello's "The Female in Ibero-America" (106). The work
       is not superseded as a bibliography by Knaster's Women in
       Spanish America (104) because its nearly 400 citations in-
       clude material on Brazil, 1975 publications, and conference
       papers and because of a separate section on research in
       progress. The essay itself includes a valuable list of
       bibliographies not repeated in the list of references.

104   _____. Women in Spanish America: An Annotated Bibliography
       from Pre-Conquest to Contemporary Times. Boston: G.K. Hall,
       1977. 696 pp.
            This major bibliography is composed of over 2,500 cita-
       tions to materials in Spanish or English published from the
       seventeenth century through 1974, unpublished doctoral dis-
       sertations, and masters' essays. Each of its fourteen

topical sections is preceded by scope notes defining its
limits and is divided into separate units on South America,
Central America, and the Caribbean. The categories chosen
cover the social sciences and humanities and, to a lesser
extent, medicine and law. Fiction and poetry are excluded
except for a few didactic examples. Writings on indigenous
women from Spanish speaking countries are included although,
as the title indicates, those on Brazilians are not.

105   PESCATELLO, ANN M. "Bibliography." In Power and Pawn: The
      Female in Iberian Families, Societies, and Cultures.
      Westport, Conn.: Greenwood Press, 1976, pp. 235-73.
         The scope of this bibliography of more than 800 items
      takes in Iberia, Iberia in Asia, Portuguese Africa, and
      pre-Conquest, Hispanic, and Brazilian America. Titles were
      selected for quality and accessibility and are in several
      European languages as well as in English. A list of special
      collections, archives, and journals precedes the alphabeti-
      cal list of published materials.

106   _____. "The Female in Ibero-America: An Essay on Research
      Bibliography and Research Directions." Latin American Re-
      search Review 7 (Summer 1972):125-41.
         The problems of research on Ibero-American women and new
      scholarship, completed or in progress, are described in this
      literature review. It is concluded by a selected annotated
      bibliography of seventy-one items, geographically arranged.
      For an update, see 103.

107   SOEIRO, SUSAN A. "Recent Work on Latin American Women: A
      Review Essay." Journal of Interamerican Studies and World
      Affairs 17 (November 1975):497-516.
         This article reviews recent literature in English in the
      disciplines of sociology, anthropology, political science,
      and history dealing with the period from colonial times to
      the present day. It cites about ninety titles, most of
      them dated between 1965 and 1974.

108   VALDÉS, NELSON P. "A Bibliography on Cuban Women in the 20th
      Century." Cuban Studies Newsletter 4 (June 1974):1-31.
         "This bibliography is limited to the socio-politico-
      economic aspects of the subject in the 20th century,
      particularly after 1959." Items included in Pescatello's
      "The Female in Ibero-America" (106) are deliberately omitted.
      The 568 citations are organized into two major divisions
      for prerevolutionary and revolutionary Cuba, each further
      divided by topic.

See also: 096, 432.

AFRICA

109 DOBERT, MARGARITA. "Women in French-speaking Africa: A
     Selected Guide to Civic and Political Participation in
     Guinea, Dahomey and Mauritania." Current Bibliography on
     African Affairs n.s. 3, no. 9 (Sept. 1970):5-21.
          Originally part of a doctoral dissertation, this work
     cites over 200 items, mostly in English or French, in an
     arrangement based on format: books, reports, periodical
     articles, newspaper articles, unpublished materials.

110 DRYDEN, PHYLLIS KAY. "Annotated Bibliography of Political
     Rights of African Women." African Law Studies 7 (1972):
     27-62.
          The first and smaller part of the bibliography consists
     of citations to published books, articles, conference
     reports, and the like, arranged by type of publication. A
     few are in French or German; most are in English. The
     larger and more valuable part lists UN treaties, resolu-
     tions, reports, programs, and conferences, together with
     evaluations of UN programs. All of these are abstracted
     at length, and the "Convention on the Political Rights of
     Women" is printed in full.

111. HAFKIN, NANCY J. Women and Development in Africa: An Anno-
     tated Bibliography. Bibliography Series, no. 1. n.p.: UN
     Economic Commission for Africa, 1977. 177 pp.
          Because it is based on the publications and holdings of
     the UNECA African Training and Research Centre for Women,
     this work is made up to an unusual degree of international
     and African government publications, although articles from
     social science journals and conference papers are also
     represented. The Centre's own publications are available
     on request; materials included in a Chicago-based microfiche
     program are marked. The nearly 600 references are grouped
     under broad subject headings. The countries considered in
     each study are listed at the close of its annotation, and
     there are country and author indexes.

112 KERINA, JANE M. "Women in Africa: A Select Bibliography."
     Africa Report 22 (Jan./Feb. 1977):44-50.
          A bibliographic essay with a list of 103 references, this
     work is "an attempt to present a sampling of accessible
     materials published since 1970 on some of the most critical
     issues relating to African women today." A few older
     classics are also included. About half the titles deal
     with African women in literature, the rest are books,
     articles, and reports studying African women.

113 KRATOCHVIL, LAURA and SHAW, SHAUNA. <u>African Women: A Select Bibliography</u>. Cambridge: African Studies Centre, 1974. 74 pp.

   This "experimental attempt at utilizing the vast amount of bibliographic material on various aspects of African studies at the African Studies Centre to provide a list of titles on a specific subject" cites 1,210 writings in a subject arrangement that includes the arts and religion as well as economic, social, and political topics. Each entry has a letter code to indicate the geographical region studied, and there are regional and author indexes.

114 MOORE, JANE ANN and OJIMBA, MARGARET. "Bibliography on Nursing and Midwifery in Africa." <u>Current Bibliography on African Affairs</u> n.s. 9, no. 2 (1976-1977):140-59.

   No explanatory material accompanies this alphabetical listing of about 400 books, articles, and reports written in English.

115 MURRAY, JOCELYN. "Women in Africa: A Select Bibliography." <u>Rural Africana</u> 29 (1975):215-29.

   "This short bibliography is assembled under five headings: (1) bibliographies; (2) social and legal status of women; (3) women's roles in ritual and religion; (4) the woman's life cycle; and (5) women in labor, employment, and economic development. It is confined to works in English and French and aims at including the 'classic' works on the topic, whatever their date of publication, but otherwise concentrates on recent work, while endeavoring to be reasonably representative."

116 PIGAULT, GÉRARD and RWEGERA, DAMIEN. <u>Mariages en Afrique sub-saharienne: Bibliographie internationale 1945-1975 établie par ordinateur/Marriages in sub-Saharan Africa: International Bibliography 1945-1975 Indexed by Computer</u>. RIC Supplement 23-26. Strasbourg: Cerdic Publications, 1975. 211 pp. Available from Cerdic, 9, Place de l'Universite, F-67084 Strasbourg-Cedex, France.

   No more than half the 2,212 citations in this bibliography of African, European, and North American books and articles are in English. Three computer produced indexes not only list the items by subject matter, country, and ethnological group but also prefix each item number with a number/letter combination which indicates the publication's format, its language, and whether it was written before or after the independence of the country with which it deals. A foreword describes this as an ongoing project.

117 WESTFALL, GLORIA D. "Nigerian Women: A Bibliographic Essay." <u>Africana Journal</u> 5 (Summer 1974):99-138.

This essay reviews books, articles, government documents, and dissertations specifically on women in Nigeria and general works containing a significant contribution on the subject. The publications covered are in English or French and were issued between 1967 and fall 1972. The article is organized around social, economic, political, and educational topics and contains a brief section on Nigerian women in literature and folkore.

See also: 096, 105, 123.

MIDDLE EAST

For additional bibliographies containing materials on women in Israel, consult the section Religion--Judaism.

118 BEIRUT. Université Saint-Joseph. Centre d'Etudes pour le Monde Arabe Moderne. <u>Arab Culture and Society in Change: A Partially Annotated Bibliography of Books and Articles in English, French, German and Italian</u>. Beirut: Dar el-Mashreq Publishers, distr. Near East Books Co., New York, 1973. 318 pp.
  Because its central theme is the encounter of modern or western culture and traditional Arab values in the Arab countries of the Middle East and North Africa from 1914 to the present, a large proportion of this bibliography has to do with women. Taken together, the sections Condition of Women, Marriage and Family, and Laws of Personal Status include nearly 500 references to books, articles, and dissertations, with another 100 cross-references to related materials in other sections.

119 GULICK, JOHN and GULICK, MARGARET E. <u>An Annotated Bibliography of Sources Concerned with Women in the Modern Muslim Middle East</u>. Princeton Near East Paper no. 17. Princeton, N.J.: Princeton University Program in Near Eastern Studies, 1974. 26 pp.
  Nearly all the titles listed in this bibliography are English-language books and articles published since 1960. Its classified arrangement includes a section on literature.

120 LYTLE, ELIZABETH. <u>Women in Israel: A Selected Bibliography</u>. Public Administration Series, no. P194. Monticello, Ill.: Vance Bibliographies, 1979. 14 pp.
  "This bibliography contains 136 citations of primarily American, British, and Israeli monographs, periodical articles, dissertations, and government documents published between 1934 and 1978. All the literature cited comes from the humanities and social sciences, especially from the

disciplines of sociology and psychology." The eighteen
categories in the topical arrangement do not include women
in religious Judaism.

121 _____. Women in Turkey: A Selected Bibliography. Public
Administration Series, no. P172. Monticello, Ill.: Vance
Bibliographies, 1979. 14 pp.
"Contained in this bibliography are 177 citations of
primarily American, British, and Turkish monographs, periodical articles, dissertations, and government documents
published between 1837 and 1976," almost all of them in
English. Since, according to the compiler, only 32 percent
were published after 1940, the chief value would appear to
be for historical research rather than for the study of
contemporary conditions.

122 MICHIGAN. University. Library. Women in the Near East: A
Booklist. Ann Arbor: 1974. 12 pp.
This "partial listing of books in the University of
Michigan Libraries about women and their status in the Near
East" is composed principally of works in Near Eastern
languages.

123 al-QAZZAZ, AYAD. Women in the Middle East and North Africa:
An Annotated Bibliography. Middle East Monographs, no. 2.
Austin: Center for Middle Eastern Studies, University of
Texas, 1977. 178 pp.
This extensively annotated selection of English language
materials seeks to represent the whole range of Islamic
position on women as expressed by both Muslim and Western
scholars. The titles listed are almost all dated between
1950 and 1976 and include a number of unpublished papers.
They are alphabetically arranged with indexes by country
and by broad topics that include Arab women in the U.S. and
in Israel.

124 RACCAGNI, MICHELLE. The Modern Arab Woman: A Bibliography.
Metuchen, N.J.: Scarecrow Press, 1978. 272 pp.
A comprehensive bibliography of nearly 3,000 items, this
work attempts to list "all books, articles, reports and
dissertations in Western languages, principally English
and French, as well as Arabic" from the early ninet enth
century (sparsely represented) to 1976. Titles of Arabic
articles are given in English. The first fifth of the work
is a subject arrangement of materials on Arab women in general, including a substantial section on Islam and Islamic
law. The rest of the volume is organized by country, with
the sections on Algeria, Egypt, Libya, Morocco, and Tunisia
further divided by topic. Literary works by and about women
are listed under these five countries as well as in the
initial general section. There are occasional brief annotations and author and subject indexes.

125 VAN DUSEN, ROXANN A. "The Study of Women in the Middle East:
Some Thoughts." Middle East Studies Association Bulletin
10 (May 1, 1976):1-19.
A reference list of 153 books, articles, documents, and
dissertations in English and French accompanies this literature review discussing published research, chiefly since
1960, and topics on which little has been written.

See also: 247.

ASIA

126 ANANDA, PETER. "Women in the Philippines: A Preliminary
Bibliography." Cormosea Newsletter 7 (1974):18-21.
The majority of the nearly 100 publications cited in
this bibliography of English language materials are of
Philippine origin. They represent a wide variety of
formats, including books, articles, pamphlets, government
documents, and theses; and their imprints extend from 1928
to 1971.

*127 Bibliography of Asian Studies. 1969- n.p.: Association
for Asian Studies. Annual.
Previously issued as part of the Journal of Asian
Studies, the bibliography is geographically arranged.
Under each area or country there is a section, Anthropology
and Sociology, and within this a subsection, Women, listing
scholarly publications on women in that geographical unit.

128 LYTLE, ELIZABETH. Women in India: A Comprehensive Bibliography. Public Administration Series, no. P109. Monticello,
Ill.: Vance Bibliographies, 1978. 29 pp.
"Contained in this bibliography are 386 citations of
primarily British, American, and Indian monographs, readings
collections, periodical articles, and government documents
published between 1881 and 1977," with half of them published since 1950. Arrangement is in over twenty topical
sections on subjects as specific as female slavery and
widowhood. Despite its title, this is the least comprehensive bibliography on women in India listed here, but it
is probably the one most readily available.

129 MARTIN, DIANA. Women in Chinese Society. Commonwealth Bureau
of Agricultural Economics Annotated Bibliography no. 28.
Farnham Royal: Commonwealth Agricultural Bureaux, 1974.
22 pp.
Mainland Chinese publications are strongly represented
in this compilation of 208 "selected references to material,
in Chinese, English, and a few in French and German, written

since the establishment of the People's Republic and
referring to areas of social, political, and economic change
in women's status since that time." Entries are grouped
by format: general books, articles from Mainland Chinese
periodicals, articles from non-Chinese periodicals, Chinese
books and documents, non-Chinese books, doctoral dissertations. All titles are given in English, with the original
language indicated. Aside from the abstracts supplied for
nineteen articles, the only annotations are occasional
scope notes.

130   PAPANEK, HANNA. "Women in South and Southeast Asia: Issues
      and Research." Signs 1 (Autumn 1975):193-214.
         The author analyzes the direction of current research
      on women in Indonesia, Bangladesh, Pakistan, and India and
      suggests areas for further investigation. Her Selected
      Bibliography of nearly seventy items, alphabetically
      arranged, contains a large proportion of unpublished papers.
      Many of these are on file in the pamphlet collection of the
      South Asia Reference Center, Regenstein Library, University
      of Chicago.

131   SAKALA, CAROL. Women of South Asia: A Guide to Resources.
      Millwood, N.Y.: Kraus-Thomson, 1980.
         The editor writes that the first part of this bibliog-
      raphy will contain about 4,500 annotated references to
      women in Bangladesh, India, Nepal, Pakistan, and Sri Lanka
      from the sixth century to the present day. Limited to
      western language materials, it will include monographs,
      articles, dissertations, periodicals, and nonprint media.
      The second part will consist of four essays on archival
      sources in India, Pakistan, Bangladesh, and England.

132   SHREEMATI NATHIBAI DAMODAR THACKERSEY WOMEN'S UNIVERSITY,
      BOMBAY. Research Unit on Women's Studies. A Select
      Bibliography on Women in India. Bombay: Allied Publishers
      [1975?] 131 pp.
         The compilers tried to cover English language books
      published up to March 1975, important journal articles from
      1960 to 1975, unpublished theses, and (to a lesser extent)
      reports. Popular magazines were excluded. Within a clas-
      sified subject arrangement, publications are listed by
      format. There is an author index.

133   VELEZ, MARIA CRISTINA. Images of the Filipina: A Bibliography.
      [Manila?] Ala-Ala Foundation, 1975. 219 pp.
         This extensive bibliography on the status and role of
      Filipino women from precolonial times to the present anno-
      tates nearly 600 references. They are grouped by type of

publication: books and scholarly articles (alphabetically by author), dissertations (chronologically), magazine articles (alphabetically by magazine title). A chronological list of writings from 1889 through 1975 includes some titles not listed in the main bibliography, and there are author and subject indexes.

134   <u>Women on the Indian Scene: An Annotated Bibliography</u>. Ed. Kalpana Dasgupta. New Delhi: Abhinav Publications, 1976. 391 pp.
    The YWCA of India sponsored the compilation of this, the most extensive bibliography to date on women in India. Its 822 entries represent English language books, reports, monographs, and periodical articles dealing with the problems and status of women in India from the ancient period to the present day and published from 1801 until June 1975. They are organized in broad subject categories and thereunder by period, and this historical approach is carried further by a prefatory essay, "Research on Status of Women in India--A Trend Survey."

See also: 105, 248.

AUSTRALIA AND NEW ZEALAND

135   BUNKLE, PHILLIDA. "Bibliography" in <u>Learning about Sexism in New Zealand</u>. Ed. Phillida Bunkle, Stephen Levine, and Christopher Wainright. Wellington: Learmonth Publications, 1976, pp. 232-255. (Available from Christopher Wainright, 25 Taylor Rd., Claremont, Western Australia.)

136   GEPP, MERYL JULIE. <u>Australian Women, 1952-March 1975: A Bibliography of Articles on Women's Place in Australian Society</u>. State Library of South Australia, Reference Services Bibliographies, no. 2/75. Adelaide: Libraries Board of South Australia, 1975. 63 pp.

137   REED, JANET, et al. "Sources on Women" in <u>Women at Work</u>. Special Project no. 3. Canberra: Australian Society for the Study of Labour History, 1975, pp. 146-57. Issued as <u>Labour History</u>, no. 29, 1975.
    Eight authors in all were responsible for this assortment: a description of the then unpublished Australian archives guide (046), a bibliographic essay on recent journal articles on women (principally women in Australia), and reviews of five books on women in Australia.

138   SUMMERS, ANNE. "Bibliography: Women in Australia," <u>Refractory Girl</u>, no. 1 (Summer 1972-73), pp. 32-35; no. 2 (Autumn 1973), pp. 30-37; no. 3 (Winter 1973), pp. 34-43.

See also: 045.

41

Topical Subjects

This section lists bibliographies dealing with topical subjects
either cross-culturally or in the context of U.S. society. A bibliography on a topical subject within one country or area (other than
the U.S.) is listed in the section for that country under Geographical
Subjects, with a cross-reference under topic.

HISTORY

Most of the bibliographies listed under Geographical Subjects include
materials on the history of women within the area with which they are
concerned.

See also the topical sections History of Education, Labor History,
History of the Family, and Witchcraft.

General

139   DAVIS, NATALIE ZEMON and CONWAY, JILL K. Society and the
      Sexes: A Bibliography of Women's History of Early Modern
      Europe, Colonial America, and the United States. New York:
      Garland Publishing, forthcoming.

140   ROWBOTHAM, SHEILA. Women's Liberation and Revolution: A
      Bibliography. 2d ed. Bristol, England: Falling Wall
      Press, 1973. 24 pp.
          Some 300 "books, pamphlets and articles which explore
      the relationship between feminism and revolutionary
      politics" in western Europe, Russia, China, and the U.S.
      are cited in this annotated bibliography. Although it is
      now dated (its coverage of the Women's Liberation Movement
      ends at February 1972), it is still valuable for its rad-
      ical perspective on women's history.

United States

141   COMMON WOMAN COLLECTIVE. <u>Women in U.S. History: An Annotated
        Bibliography</u>. Cambridge, Mass.: The Collective, 1976.
        114 pp. (Available from Goddard-Cambridge, 186 Hampshire
        St., Cambridge, MA 02139.)
           A highly selective listing, one of whose purposes was to
make information on women's history available to non-
academics, this bibliography has its chief value in the
compilers' socialist-feminist perspective, reflected in
the evaluative annotations and in the large proportion of
material on Third World and working class women. The
detailed subject arrangement of thirty-five categories is
provided with abundant cross-references.

142   FOX, VICKI G. and STOECKEL, ALTHEA L. "The Role of Women in
        the American Revolution: An Annotated Bibliography."
        <u>Indiana Social Studies Quarterly</u> 28 (Spring 1975):14-29.
           About eighty primary and secondary sources, dramas, and
children's books are listed in four sections: background
materials on women in Revolutionary America, biographies,
reprints of women's eyewitness accounts of the Revolution,
and Bicentennial publications.

143   KRICHMAR, ALBERT. <u>The Women's Rights Movement in the United
        States, 1848-1970: A Bibliography and Sourcebook</u>. Met-
        uchen, N.J.: Scarecrow Press, 1972. 436 pp.
           Since, by the editor's own statement, the "topics covered
concern the legal, political, economic, religious, educational, and professional status of women since 1848," it
is best considered a general bibliography on the history of
women in this country. The work is made up of over 5,000
references to books, articles, and government documents in
a subject arrangement with author and subject indexes, a
chapter describing over 400 manuscript sources with its own
index, and a list of "Women's Liberation Serial Publications"
with its index. Especially noteworthy is the subject section
on biography, where one can find lists of references on a
number of women not included in <u>Notable American Women</u> and
therefore difficult to research.

144   LERNER, GERDA. <u>Bibliography in the History of American Women</u>.
        3d revision. Bronxville, N.Y.: Sarah Lawrence College,
        1978. 79 pp.
           Lerner, a pioneer in the women's studies movement, began
this work as a reading list for her students and has now
announced that this is the last edition she will undertake
because of the explosion of publication in the area. In
spite of the interdisciplinary nature of much recent scholarship in women's history, the list is restricted as closely
as possible to historical works. They include older books
and articles as well as recent materials and are arranged
in broad subject categories.

145   SICHERMAN, BARBARA. "Review Essay: American History." <u>Signs</u>
       1 (Winter 1975):461-85.
            Works published between September 1973 and May 1975 are
       covered in this survey of new trends in the study of Ameri-
       can women, which focuses largely on the nineteenth century.
       A number of the seventy-nine footnotes cite more than one
       title, and there is a list of twenty-four additional
       readings.

146   <u>Women in American History</u>. Ed. Cynthia Harrison. Santa
       Barbara, Calif.: ABC-Clio Press, forthcoming.
            The publisher describes this as consisting of 1,800-2,000
       abstracts drawn from the data base of <u>America: History and
       Life</u>, vols. 1-13, 1964-76, covering material published
       through 1975.

*147   <u>Writings on American History: A Subject Bibliography of Arti-
       cles</u>, 1962/73- Washington: American Historical Associa-
       tion, 1974- Annual.
            A section, "Women's History," regularly appears as part
       of the division on social history.

                                                        See also: 150.

<u>Canada</u>

148   STRONG-BOAG, VERONICA. "Cousin Cinderella: A Guide to His-
       torical Literature Pertaining to Canadian Women" in <u>Women
       in Canada</u>. Ed. Marylee Stephenson. Toronto: New Press,
       1973, pp. 262-90.
            The topical divisions of this bibliographic essay are:
       Autobiographies and Biographies, Demography, Marriage and
       the Family, Sexuality, Education, The Home and Domestic
       Life, Work, Organizational Involvement, Sports, Literature,
       Anti-feminism.

<u>Great Britain</u>

149   "BIBLIOGRAPHY FOR THE STUDY OF WOMEN IN ENGLISH HISTORY."
       <u>Canadian Newsletter of Research on Women</u> 6 (October 1977):
       136-45.
            The bibliography reprints selected categories from the
       reading list of a course on women in English history from
       the Middle Ages to the present day. Entries are grouped
       in chronological sections: Anglo-Saxon and medieval period,
       and the sixteenth, seventeenth, eighteenth, and nineteenth
       centuries. Some literary criticism is included among the
       books and articles listed.

150   HORNE, GRENDA. "The Liberation of British and American Women's
       History." <u>Bulletin of the Society for the Study of Labour
       History</u>, no. 26 (Spring 1973), pp. 28-39.
            This review essay deals with publications since 1950 and
       work in progress at the time. The accompanying list of
       about 150 books, articles, theses, and dissertations,
       topically arranged, is now useful chiefly for its British
       materials, especially theses and dissertations.

151   KANNER, S. BARBARA. "The Women of England in a Century of
       Social Change, 1815-1914: A Select Bibliography." In
       <u>Suffer and Be Still: Women in the Victorian Age</u>. Ed.
       Martha Vicinus. Bloomington, Indiana University Press,
       1972, pp. 173-206.

152   _____. _____. Part 2. In <u>A Widening Sphere: Changing Roles
       of Victorian Women</u>. Ed. Martha Vicinus. Bloomington:
       Indiana University Press, 1977, pp. 199-270.
            Both parts of this impressive bibliography (excerpted
       from a longer work in progress) follow generally similar
       organization: topical sections, much subdivided, are
       introduced by a bibliographic essay and list primary and
       secondary sources in chronological sequence. Part 1, citing
       500 titles, deals with employment, education, population
       and emigration, law, political activity, social service,
       and public attitudes. Part 2, citing nearly 700 titles, is
       concerned with domestic questions, especially marriage,
       family, and health, but also the applications of science
       and social science and women's organizations. It is impor-
       tant not to overlook the notes, which contain a number of
       citations not included in the bibliography proper.

153   PALMEGIANO, E. M. <u>Women and British Periodicals, 1832-1867:
       A Bibliography</u>. New York: Garland Publishing, 1976.
       118 pp.
            Three checklists make up the bibliographic part of this
       volume. The first gives basic information, including
       editors' names and location of most complete holdings, for
       eighty-five periodicals issued for women readers. (No
       access to the periodicals' contents is provided.) The
       second cites nonfiction articles dealing with women in 171
       periodicals intended for general readership, and the third
       lists 68 periodicals giving no information about women.
       A lengthy introduction analyzes the stereotypes of women
       and men found in these journals. The checklists, but not
       the introduction, originally appeared in <u>Victorian
       Periodicals Newsletter</u> 9 (March 1976):1-36.

154   SCHNORRENBERG, BARBARA BRANDON. "Toward a Bibliography of
       Eighteenth-Century Englishwomen." <u>Eighteenth-Century Life</u>
       1, no. 3 (1975):50-52.

This bibliographic essay is limited to books not listed in the two volumes of Bibliography of British History dealing with the eighteenth century. Contemporary publications, collections of letters, diaries and memoirs, and works on literature are excluded. The titles cited range in date from 1879 to 1972 and include a number of biographies of individual women.

155   The Women of England from Anglo-Saxon Times to the Present: Interpretive Bibliographical Essays. Ed. Barbara Kanner. Hamden, Conn.: Archon Books, 1979. 429 pp.
       Each of the dozen essays in this collection has both notes and a bibliography of the works discussed, in most cases amounting to 150 references or more. Two chapters are devoted to historiography and archival sources. The others are concerned with women in general or with one historical approach to their lives during particular historical periods from Anglo-Saxon times to the twentieth century. There is a subject index.

See also: 180, 184.

Europe

156   ERICKSON, CAROLLY and CASEY, KATHLEEN. "Women in the Middle Ages: A Working Bibliography." Mediaeval Studies 37 (1975):340-59.
       The compilers state that their list "attempts to acknowledge the new orientations that have emerged in the last decade while preserving the most valuable older works." They cite nearly 350 scholarly books and articles written in English, French, German, and Italian in a topical arrangement of nine categories, of which the largest is concerned with marriage alliance and descent.

157   GOODWATER, LEANNA. Women in Antiquity: An Annotated Bibliography. Metuchen, N.J.: Scarecrow Press, 1975. 171 pp.
       The women with whom this bibliography is concerned are those of ancient Greece and Rome, including Minoans, Etruscans, and women of the Hellenistic kingdoms and some of the provinces of the Roman Empire, from the earliest recorded history to 476 A.D. The treatment of women in literature is considered as well as the legal, political, and social aspects of their lives, and both classical sources and modern studies are cited, with the aim of being comprehensive in modern works in English and selective in those in Greek, Latin, French, German, and Italian. Biographies of individuals make up a large part of the works cited; these lists are as complete as possible except for Sappho and Cleopatra.

158 KELLY, JOAN. <u>Bibliography in the History of European Women</u>.
4th revision. Bronxville, N.Y.: Sarah Lawrence College,
1976. 132 pp. Available from Women's Studies Program,
Sarah Lawrence College, Bronxville, N.Y. 10708, also as
microfiche only from EDRS, ED 155 106.

   Designed primarily for students and with further revi-
sions anticipated, this extensive reading list cites few
foreign sources but includes older works as well as recent
ones. After a series of topical sections, such as women in
literature and women and religion, that cover more than one
historical period, the organization is basically chronological. Most of the period divisions include a subsection of
biography.

159 OFFEN, KAREN M. "The 'Woman Question' as a Social Issue in
Nineteenth-Century France: A Bibliographical Essay."
<u>Third Republic/Troisième République</u>, no. 3/4 (Spring/Fall
1977), pp. 238-99.

   The author describes her intent as "an interim report on
the most useful published books and articles, both old and
new, pertaining to the history of women in France during
the nineteenth and early twentieth centuries." Topics
considered include demography, legal position, images of
woman's nature and family role, education, employment, and
feminism. The historical period covered by different
topical sections varies, in some cases extending as late as
World War II.

160 POMEROY, SARAH B. "Selected Bibliography on Women in Antiquity."
<u>Arethusa</u> 6 (Spring 1973):125-57.

   The three elements making up this article are a bibliographic essay, the syllabus for an undergraduate course on
women in classical antiquity, and a basic reading list for
nonclassicists unfamiliar with standard classical reference
books and texts. The very selective bibliographic essay
covers Bronze Age and classical Greece, the Hellenistic
period, ancient Rome, and early Christianity, citing works
in English and "languages commonly read by classicists."
Emphasis throughout is sociological rather than literary
because there are already bibliographies for most classical
authors, and the anthropological titles listed, especially
in the case of Bronze Age Greece, are a particular strong
point. Also noteworthy is the section on women under
Christianity written by Michael Southwell.

161 SOWERWINE, CHARLES. "Women, Socialism, and Feminism, 1872-
1922: A Bibliography." <u>Third Republic/Troisième République</u>,
no. 3/4 (Spring/Fall 1977), pp. 300-366.

   The first part of this bibliography cites the writings
of French socialist women militants and of feminists with

whom they were associated. Part 2 names the feminist and
socialist women's periodicals for the period, and Part 3
is a series of chronological lists of French and international socialist and feminist congresses, with an indication
of the degree of women's participation in each socialist
congress and any resolutions on the woman question that it
passed. An introductory essay identifies individual women
and defines their type of activity.

LITERATURE

This section includes both bibliographies on the image of women in
literature and those concerned with a number of women authors. No
bibliographies on individual women authors are cited here, however,
since there are a great many of them and they are readily located
elsewhere.

General

*162   Bibliography of Literature in English by and about Women [for
        1974]- Women and Literature, supp. to the Fall issue,
        1975- Annual.
            Bibliographies for 1974-76 were edited by Florence Boos,
        those for 1977- by Lynn F. Miller. Title and scope have
        varied somewhat; the latest issue examined is titled 1977
        Bibliography of Literature in English by and about Women:
        600-1975 and includes about 1,200 citations to works pub-
        lished in Great Britain, U.S., Africa, Canada, India,
        Australia, and some European and Latin American countries.
        Items are listed in a decimal classification arranged by
        country and thereunder by period and genre, with works by
        an author and criticism of them grouped together. There
        are occasional brief annotations, and book reviews are
        identified as such. This is by far the most comprehensive
        bibliography on the subject.

163   HAGEMAN, ELIZABETH H. "Images of Women in Renaissance Litera-
        ture: A Selected Bibliography of Scholarship." Women's
        Studies Newsletter 5 (Spring 1977):15-17.
            About seventy-five books, articles, and dissertations with
        dates from the early twentieth century through 1976 were
        selected for this bibliography. Its topical organization
        includes a section on the classical and medieval background
        as well as sections on the social and intellectual history
        and the literature of the sixteenth and seventeenth
        centuries.

164   LEWIS, LINDA K.   "Women in Literature: A Selected Bibliography."
       Bulletin of Bibliography 35 (July/Sept. 1978):116-22, 131.
            This list contains about 250 of the more important books,
       essays, and articles on the image of women in literature
       written in English at any time from the nineteenth century
       through fall 1977, the majority during the 1960s and 1970s.
       Titles published between 1970 and 1975 are included only if
       they do not appear in Women in Literature: Criticism of
       the Seventies (165).

165   MYERS, CAROL FAIRBANKS.   Women in Literature: Criticism of
       the Seventies.   Metuchen, N.J.:   Scarecrow Press, 1976.
       256 pp.

166   FAIRBANKS, CAROL.   More Women in Literature: Criticism of the
       Seventies.   Metuchen, N.J.:   Scarecrow Press, 1979.   457 pp.
            Both volumes seek to provide a selected bibliography of
       books, periodical articles, and dissertations relating to
       women characters in literature, feminist literary criticism,
       and women writers of any period or country (although the
       references included are almost exclusively in English).
       The first cites publications from 1970 through spring 1975
       and covers about 300 writers; the second cites publications
       from 1970 through 1977, covering about 1,000 writers.   The
       greater part of each volume is taken up with references
       concerned with individual writers; a shorter section of
       each is a general bibliography having to do with periods or
       genres or with some aspect of the study of women in litera-
       ture.   Unfortunately, this general bibliography is arranged
       alphabetically according to the author of the critical work
       cited, with no subject approach provided.   There is an index
       of critics and editors.

167   SCHIBANOFF, SUSAN.   "Images of Women in Medieval Literature:
       A Selected Bibliography."   Women's Studies Newsletter 4
       (Fall 1976):10-11.
            This partially annotated bibliography cites about fifty
       items in a classified arrangement.   The books and articles
       listed include studies on classical literature (by way of
       background), general medieval studies, and literary studies
       on Chaucer, other medieval authors, and women in folklore
       and proverbs.

168   SCHWARTZ, NARDA LACEY.   Articles on Women Writers: A Bibliog-
       raphy.   Santa Barbara, Calif.:   ABC-Clio Press, 1977.
       236 pp.
            The more than 600 women authors included are those of
       any period from the U.S., Great Britain, Ireland, Australia,
       New Zealand, and Africa who wrote in English and were the
       subject of at least one article other than a book review

published between 1960 and 1975. The articles listed were located through a search of twenty-one serial bibliographies and <u>Dissertation Abstracts International</u> and represent both scholarly and popular literature. The citations for each writer are divided into bibliographies, general works, and criticism of individual works. Articles dealing with more than one writer are listed in full under each one. There is an author index.

169   <u>Women and Literature: An Annotated Bibliography of Women Writers</u>. 3d ed. Cambridge, Mass.: Women and Literature Collective, 1976. 212 pp. Available from the Collective, P.O. Box 441, Cambridge, MA 02138.

The compilers "have sought to correct the imbalance caused by a phallocentric culture and criticism by providing information about women's writing from a feminist perspective," and this approach gives the work its unique value. Most of the 819 entries are works of fiction, and two-thirds of them are listed in the sections on British and American writing. The international section, subdivided by country, lists only titles for which there are English translations available. Brief sections of anthologies and works about literature complete the volume. Besides the evaluative annotations, there are biographical sketches of selected authors, a subject index focusing on feminist concerns, and an author index.

See also: 473, 474, 475.

American

170   <u>American Women Writers: A Critical Reference Guide</u>. Ed. Lina Mainiero. New York: Frederick Ungar, forthcoming. Vol. 1, A-E has been announced for 1979.

171   BAKERMAN, JANE S. and DeMARR, MARY JEAN. <u>Adolescent Female Images in American Novels: An Annotated Bibliography</u>. New York: Garland Publishing, forthcoming.

172   GHERMAN, DAWN LANDER. "Frontier and Wilderness: American Women Authors." <u>University of Michigan Papers in Women's Studies</u> 2, no. 2 (1976):7-38.

American women of all races who wrote about their experiences in the wilderness from the colonial period through the nineteenth century are the subject of this annotated bibliography and guide to research. Over 200 primary sources and 19 works of secondary literature are listed in separate sections, followed by a list of bibliographies consulted and a series of notes on captivity narratives, secondary sources, and fiction.

173 HUDDLESTON, EUGENE L. "Feminist Verse Satire in America: A
     Checklist, 1700-1800." Bulletin of Bibliography 32 (July
     1975):115-21, 132.
          The aim of the checklist is to include "all feminist
     satire of the eighteenth century published in American
     books and magazines, regardless of the author's nationality."
     The 220 items are listed in a classed arrangement, with
     brief descriptive annotations and with authors known or
     assumed to be British marked with an asterisk.

174 REARDON, JOAN and THORSEN, KRISTINE A. Poetry by American
     Women, 1900-1975: A Bibliography. Metuchen, N.J.: Scare-
     crow Press, 1979. 674 pp.
          This is an alphabetical listing of more than 5,500
     women poets of U.S. citizenship whose major works appeared
     from 1900 through 1975 and who published at least one
     separate volume of verse. Birth and death dates are sup-
     plied in about half the cases. Each woman's poetical works,
     including verse for children, are listed chronologically
     with full citation including pagination. Editions other
     than the first are not necessarily included, and the terms
     of the title exclude any works that a poet might have pub-
     lished before 1900. A title index is provided.

175 WHITE, BARBARA A. American Women Writers: An Annotated Bib-
     liography of Criticism. New York: Garland Publishing,
     1977. 126 pp.
          The criticism cited in this work is solely that concerned
     with women writers as a group or with three or more writers
     of fiction, poetry, or drama. Most of it originated in the
     U.S. and was published before 1976. Newspaper articles and
     dissertations are excluded. The 413 citations are grouped
     into subject categories: Biography, Special Groups, Special
     Topics, Literary History, Contemporary Assessments, Feminine
     Sensibility, Problems, Phallic Criticism, Feminist Literary
     Criticism, Miscellaneous. Each section concludes with cross-
     references tying together related materials in different
     sections, and there is a personal name index to critics and
     editors.

See also: 069, 183, 434, 439.

Canadian

176 ANTHONY, GERALDINE and USMIANI, TINA. "A Bibliography of
     English Canadian Drama Written by Women." World Literature
     Written in English 17 (April 1978):120-43.
          This alphabetical listing lacks any introductory material
     to explain the basis for inclusion. The works cited appear
     to include both the plays themselves, as separate publica-
     tions, in anthologies, or in periodicals, and also the
     reference works used in identifying them. Plays listed date
     from the mid-nineteenth century through 1977.

177 HAMEL, RÉGINALD. <u>Bibliographie sommaire sur l'histoire de</u>
<u>l'écriture féminine au Canada (1769-1961)</u>. Montréal:
Université de Montréal, 1974. 134 pp.
Since this selective bibliography is concerned only with
the literature of French Canadian women and its backgrounds,
it is not surprising that the works cited are, almost with--
out exception, in French. About half its length is devoted
to general materials on women and the family in Canada,
including books, articles from journals unlikely to be
indexed elsewhere, and even an occasional poem or archival
collection. The rest of the work consists of separate
lists of novels (with English translations noted), young
adult fiction, and poetry.

178 LINDEN, MARJORIE and TEEPLE, DIANE. "The Evolving Role of
Canadian Women Writers." <u>Ontario Library Review</u> 61 (June
1977):114-31.
The principal focus of this bibliography is on fiction,
with some representative prose writing but no poetry
included. It covers both English Canadian authors and
French Canadians whose works are readily available in
English. The basis for selection is the interest of what
the writer has to say about the role of women in Canada,
rather than intrinsic literary merit. Authors are grouped
within period divisions, with an author's works, selected
criticism, book reviews, and bibliographies listed in that
order.

179 McINTYRE, SHEILA. "A Bibliography of Scholarship on Literature
by and about Canadian Women." <u>Canadian Newsletter of Re-</u>
<u>search on Women</u> 6 (February 1977):99-114.
Over 200 references to books, articles, and dissertations
published from 1972 through 1976 (plus a few especially
significant older titles) are contained in this bibliography,
which is concerned with both literature written by Canadian
women and the image of women in Canadian literature in
general.

English

180 BACKSCHEIDER, PAULA; NUSSBAUM, FELICITY; and ANDERSON,
PHILIP B. <u>An Annotated Bibliography of Twentieth-Century</u>
<u>Critical Studies of Women and Literature, 1660-1800</u>. New
York: Garland Publishing, 1977. 287 pp.
Over 1,500 references to scholarly books, articles, and
a few dissertations published between 1900 and 1975 are
contained in this bibliography on women in Restoration and
eighteenth century England. Although more literary studies
are included than any other type, its scope is not entirely

limited to literature. The first part is composed of
general studies on an assortment of social, cultural, and
historical topics. Part 2 lists genre studies, arranged
by type: biography, conduct books, drama, fiction, periodicals, poetry, with special notice given to women in the
works of six major male authors of the period. Part 3
cites writings on sixty-five outstanding women--writers,
actresses, and other notables--with a final section on
individual women for whom only a few studies were found.
An index to Restoration and eighteenth century women and
an author index complete the work.

181   FULLARD, JOYCE and SCHUELLER, RHODA WALGREN. "Eighteenth
       Century Poets: A Bibliography of Women Not Listed in the
       CBEL." Mary Wollstonecraft Journal 2 (May 1974):40-43.
           This is a list of the writings of thirty-five women not
       represented in the Cambridge Bibliography of English Litera-
       ture. It is followed (pp. 44-46) by an article by Fullard
       on the representation of eighteenth century women poets in
       anthologies.

182   GARTENBERG, PATRICIA and WHITTEMORE, NENA THAMES. "Checklist
       of English Women in Print, 1475-1640." Bulletin of Bibliog-
       raphy 34 (Jan. 1977):1-13.
           Not only separately printed books written by English
       women but also short writings included in collective works
       and foreign literature translated by women are included in
       this comprehensive bibliography. The STC number is given
       for writings listed in the Short Title Catalogue, and the
       source of titles identified through other bibliographies is
       stated.

183   GILLESPIE, DIANE F. "The Female Artist in British and American
       Literature: Overview and Checklist." Modernist Studies 1,
       no. 3 (1974-75):39-50.

184   GRECO, NORMA and NOVOTNY, RONAELE. "Bibliography of Women in
       the English Renaissance." University of Michigan Papers
       in Women's Studies 1 (June 1974):29-57.
           Described as "an annotated listing of Renaissance and
       twentieth-century publications dealing with English women,
       1500-1623," this work is concerned with women's relation-
       ship to the literature of the period and, to a lesser
       extent, with their social history. Its major divisions
       comprise works by women writers and criticism of those
       works, women in relation to male writers, female characters
       in relation to real or ideal women of the times, and women
       in cultural and historical context. This last section
       includes a number of biographies of individual women.

185   TRAVITSKY, BETTY. "The New Mother of the English Renaissance
      (1489-1659): A Descriptive Catalogue." Bulletin of Re-
      search in the Humanities, in press.

Other National Literatures

186   BILLICK, DAVID J. "Women in Hispanic Literature: A Checklist
      of Doctoral Dissertations and Master's Theses, 1905-1975."
      Women Studies Abstracts 6 (Summer 1977):1-11.

187   _____. "Theses and Dissertations on Women in Hispanic Litera-
      ture: A Supplement for 1976-77." Women Studies Abstracts
      7 (Summer/Fall 1978):1-3.
          These are international checklists based on a search of
      a number of general, topical, regional, and institutional
      lists. Studies on the literature of Spain are arranged by
      period, and there are separate sections for Latin American
      and (in the supplement only) Portuguese literature.

188   BOULLATA, KAMAL. "Bibliography" in Women of the Fertile
      Crescent: An Anthology of Modern Poetry by Arab Women.
      Washington: Three Continents Press, 1978, pp. 221-50.
          This selected bibliography on Arab women focuses on their
      poetry and other literature, citing books, articles, dis-
      sertations, and unpublished papers, mainly in English, but
      with some outstanding titles in Arabic or French. Most of
      the references appeared between 1950 and 1975. They are
      organized in categories that include general works, works
      on Arab women and literature, modern fiction by Arab women
      in translation, anthologies containing modern poetry by
      Arab women in translation, and published works of Arab
      women poets (divided by country). There is also a listing
      of Arab women poets who published in literary periodicals
      between 1950 and 1975, without indication of which periodi-
      cals are covered.

189   COMMISSIONG, BARBARA and THORPE, MARJORIE. "A Select Bibliog-
      raphy of Women Writers in the Eastern Caribbean (Excluding
      Guyana)." World Literature Written in English 17 (April
      1978):279-304.
          Criteria for selection are not given, but the titles
      included in this bibliography represent English language
      poetry, short stories, novels and drama published separately
      or as a part of an anthology or periodical, chiefly since
      1960. Citations are listed according to literary genre
      within geographical divisions: Antigua, Barbados, Dominica,
      Grenada, Montserrat, St. Kitts, St. Vincent, Trinidad/Tobago.

190   McNAB, UTE. "Bibliography of German Literary Feminism, 1865-
      1914." Canadian Newsletter of Research on Women 5 (May
      1976):59-91.

Originally the bibliography for a doctoral dissertation, this is an alphabetical listing without commentary.

191 MARKS, ELAINE. "Review Essay: Women and Literature in France." Signs 3 (Summer 1978):832-42.
      In this survey of French literary criticism from 1969 through 1978 citations appear only in the forty-two foot-notes, many of which contain several titles.

192 O'QUINN, KATHLEEN. Latin American Women Authors: A Bio-Bibliography. Boston: G.K. Hall, forthcoming.

193 SCHMIDT, NANCY J. "African Women Writers of Literature for Children." World Literature Written in English 17 (April 1978):7-21.
      A bibliographic essay precedes the alphabetical list of about sixty items, including both juvenile literature in English written by African women and critical works about these authors.

194 STRAUSS, JENNIFER. "An Annotated Bibliography of Contemporary Women Poets of Australia." World Literature Written in English 17 (April 1978):63-82.
      The compiler has attempted a comprehensive listing of all poets who have published a book (other than children's verse) since 1960. For each of the eighty-four women represented, the bibliography gives citations to published books, titles of periodicals and anthologies in which she has appeared, and often a short paragraph describing her poetry and any other writing she has done.

See also: 112, 434.

Feminist Literary Criticism

195 KAPLAN, SYDNEY JANET. "Review Essay: Literary Criticism." Signs 4 (Spring 1979):514-27.
      This essay reviews scholarly writing for the period 1975-1978 having to do with women and the literary tradi-tion, individual women poets and novelists, and feminist literary criticism. References appear only in the forty-seven footnotes, many of which include several titles.

196 KOLODNY, ANNETTE. "Review Essay: Literary Criticism." Signs 2 (Winter 1976):404-21.
      This essay reviews books published in 1975, including biographies and collected letters of women writers, critical studies of individual authors, and feminist literary criti-cism. The article succeeds that by Showalter (198) and omits any titles included by her. Citations appear only as footnotes.

197   REGISTER, CHERI.   "American Feminist Literary Criticism: A
        Bibliographic Introduction."   In Feminist Literary Criti-
        cism: Explorations in Theory.   Ed. Josephine Donovan.
        Lexington: University Press of Kentucky, 1975, pp. 1–28.
            Extensive examples are offered in this description of
        three subdivisions of feminist literary criticism: analysis
        of the image of women, usually in works by male authors;
        examination of existing criticism of women writers; criti-
        cism attempting to set feminist standards for literature.
        Citations appear only in the eighty-two notes.

198   SHOWALTER, ELAINE.   "Review Essay: Literary Criticism."
        Signs 1 (Winter 1975):435–60.
            This survey for the period 1970–1975 considers the
        topics: major and minor writers, literary history, language
        and style, themes and images, and psychological approaches.
        References appear only in the eighty-three footnotes, many
        of them containing several citations.

199   STANSBURY, SHERRY A.   "A Bibliography of Feminist Criticism."
        Canadian Newsletter of Research on Women 6 (May 1977):84–114.
            Feminist criticism of art in general as well as of lit-
        erature is the concern of this bibliography.   Citations to
        English-language materials, principally by British and
        American authors, are organized in topical sections on
        literary criticism, linguistics, fine arts, and media, and
        sections by type of material, including biography, special
        issues of periodicals, conferences, anthologies, and bib-
        liographies.

See also: 190.

Children's Literature and Textbooks

Only bibliographies of studies dealing with sexism and children's
books are listed in this section.   Bibliographies of nonsexist
children's books are excluded.

200   KINGSTON, ALBERT J. and LOVELACE, TERRY.   "Sexism and Reading:
        A Critical Review of the Literature."   Reading Research
        Quarterly 13, no. 1 (1977–78):133–61.
            The authors criticize seventy-eight articles investigating
        sexism in textbooks and children's literature for the cri-
        teria used by the researchers, their concern only with the
        perpetuation of stereotypes, and their failure to consider
        the effect on children's motivation and learning.   They
        provide an elaborate table of criteria used in these arti-
        cles and a concluding list of nearly 100 references that
        includes some related studies as well as those analyzed.

201 MacLEOD, JENNIFER S. and SILVERMAN, SANDRA T. "Sexism in Textbooks: An Annotated Source List of 150+ Studies and Remedies." In You Won't Do: What Textbooks on U.S. Government Teach High School Girls. Pittsburgh: KNOW, 1973, pp. 92-109. Also available as microfiche only from EDRS, ED 091 225.

The compilers state that they omitted articles containing only basic information but tried to include any useful study or remedy. Over sixty of the titles listed are studies, many of them in progress or unpublished at the time. (Mailing addresses are provided in such cases.) The remedies include affirmative actions, clearinghouses, conferences, guidelines, and other assorted materials on sexism in education.

202 PASTINE, MAUREEN. Articles on Non-Sexist, Non-Racist Children's Literature. 1975. 27 pp. Available from EDRS, ED 117 654.

This mistitled work actually includes more than articles, as it lists in successive sections over 150 articles, 15 ERIC documents, 19 alternative publishers of children's books, 15 indexes and abstracts, 33 sources of reviews of children's books, and nearly 150 books or pamphlets.

203 PUGLIESE, PAMELA PATTERSON and CHIPLEY, DONALD R. Sexual Bias in Children's Books: Annotated Bibliography and Comparative Study. 1976. 39 pp. Available from EDRS, ED 139 007.

From the many studies of sex bias in children's literature conducted since 1970, the authors have chosen thirty-three as significantly representative. The annotation for each of these analyzes it in terms of purpose, procedure, and findings. In addition, a letter prefixed to each citation identifies its focus as being library books (fiction), textbooks, or both.

See also: 193.

MASS MEDIA

204 FRANZWA, HELEN. "The Image of Women in Television: An Annotated Bibliography." In Hearth and Home: Images of Women in the Mass Media. Ed. Gaye Tuchman, Arlene Kaplan Daniels, and James Benét. New York: Oxford University Press, 1978, pp. 273-99.

Research studies, public interest reports, and popular articles are all represented in this bibliography on the portrayal of women in television programs and its impact on attitudes and behavior.

205 FRIEDMAN, LESLIE J. Sex Role Stereotyping in the Mass Media: An Annotated Bibliography. New York: Garland Publishing, 1977. 324 pp.

Over a thousand print and nonprint items--books, articles, documents, reports, slides, films, and records--are listed in this bibliography aimed primarily at college students but also useful to scholars and professionals. (The feminist compiler aimed at impartiality but was able to locate only twelve articles defending sexism!) Titles are grouped in subject chapters whose topics include mass media in general, advertising, broadcast media, film, print media, popular culture, the image of minority group women and of men, children's media, and the impact of media stereotypes on occupational choices. There are author and subject indexes and generous cross-references.

206 KOWALSKI, ROSEMARY RIBICH. Women and Film: A Bibliography. Metuchen, N.J.: Scarecrow Press, 1976. 278 pp.
      This is a retrospective, tersely annotated bibliography of 2,302 references to books and articles. Although there are a number of items dating as far back as the 1920s and a number in foreign languages, the emphasis is on English-language materials of recent date. The organization is in four chapters: Women as Performers, Women as Film-makers, Images of Women, and Women Columnists and Critics, with a subject index that includes personal names, topical subjects, and film titles. This work should be used in conjunction with Mel Schuster's bibliography Motion Picture Performers, since Kowalski excludes magazine articles on actresses for the period (1900-1969) covered by Schuster but includes their names in her subject index, referring the reader to the item number assigned to Schuster's work.

207 TUCHMAN, GAYE. "Review Essay: Women's Depiction by the Mass Media." Signs 4 (Spring 1979):528-42.
      Maintaining that "students of the media's presentation of women have been more politically sophisticated than theoretically sound," the author reviews the background of academic study of mass communications and recent work on the portrayal of women, the reasons for media's sexism, and its effects. Citations for the studies considered, including several other literature reviews, appear only in the fifty-four footnotes, most of which contain several titles.

See also: 199, 213, 348.

FINE ARTS

208 BACHMANN, DONNA G. and PILAND, SHERRY. Women Artists: An Historical, Contemporary and Feminist Bibliography. Metuchen, N.J.: Scarecrow Press, 1978. 323 pp.

Photographers, ceramicists, and textile workers, as well as painters, sculptors, and architects are covered in this partially annotated bibliography. The first chapter, general works concerning women artists, is divided into sections for books (a category that includes microfilm collections, dissertations, and slide sets), periodical articles, and exhibition catalogs. The second and largest chapter is devoted to individual women artists from the fifteenth through the twentieth centuries. For each artist there is a brief biographical sketch and a list of references, in many cases including collections in which her work is represented. A selected list of thirty-nine books and articles on needlework makes up the final chapter.

209   COERR, S. DeRENNE. Art by Women: A Happy Hunting Bibliography. San Francisco: the author, 1978. 4 pp. Available from S. D. Coerr, 479 34th Ave., San Francisco, CA 94121.
       One section of this introductory bibliography is engagingly titled "smorgasbord," a term that might be applied to the whole, which manages to compress into two fan-folded sheets the entries for nearly 200 books, exhibition catalogs, special periodical issues, women's art journals, periodical articles, organizations, and miscellaneous publications, with brief annotations where titles are not self-explanatory. The emphasis is on women artists as a group and not on individuals.

210   Female Artists, Past and Present. 2d ed. Berkeley, Calif.: Women's History Research Center, 1974. 158 pp.

211   _____. International Women's Year 1975 Supplement. Berkeley, Calif.: Women's History Research Center, 1975. 71 pp.
       This work combines the features of a directory and bibliography for contemporary women artists and other women in the visual arts, such as teachers, critics, and museum personnel. Information given for a woman may include address, primary and secondary writings, exhibitions, illustration credits, and even a personal statement (rarely all of these). Each volume also contains a short section on female artists in art history. The supplement updates information since April 1974, adds sections on Soviet artists and on architecture, and contains the name index for both volumes.

212   FINE, ELSA HONIG; GELLMAN, LOLA B.; and LOEB, JUDY. Women's Studies and the Arts. n.p.: Women's Caucus for Art, 1978. 165 pp. Available from Elsa Honig Fine, 7008 Sherwood Drive, Knoxville, TN 37919.
       The syllabi for twenty-nine courses concerned primarily with women and the visual arts make up this collection.

Those with reading lists long enough to provide substantial bibliographies include courses on women artists in Western history, women in planning and design, and the history and sociology of American needlework.

213 Guide to Women's Art Organizations: Groups/Activities/Networks/ Publications. Ed. Cynthia Navaretta. New York: Midmarch Associates, 1979. 84 pp. Available from Women Artists News, Box 3304, Grand Central Station, New York, N.Y. 10017.
     The largest part of this book is a directory of organizations, arranged geographically within separate chapters for visual arts, architecture, design, film and video, dance, music, theater, and writing. Since the publications of many of these groups are noted, this section should not be overlooked as a source of bibliographic information. The bibliography proper (pp. 65-76) follows the same arrangement, listing books, periodicals, articles, and special issues separately within each subject category. There are succinct annotations for most titles, and out-of-print works are noted.

214 HOFFBERG, JUDITH A. "The Women Artists' Books: A Select Bibliography." Chrysalis 5 (1978):85-87.
     This is a listing of about 150 books printed since 1960 that were created by women artists as works of art in themselves. The citations, alphabetically arranged, include brief descriptions of format.

215 KRASILOVSKY, ALEXIS RAFAEL. "Feminism in the Arts: An Interim Bibliography." Artforum 10 (June 1972):72-75.
     This annotated compilation of about 100 references arranged in separate sections for articles, general works, and exhibition catalogs is not a bibliography on women artists, but rather just what the title says it is.

216 ORENSTEIN, GLORIA FEMAN. "Review Essay: Art History." Signs 1 (Winter 1975):505-25.
     This survey article covers publications for the period 1972-1975 in the fields of feminist art history and art criticism, art exhibitions, and studies of the position of women in the art marketplace and in art-related professions. About thirty references appear as footnotes or in the text.

217 WEATHERFORD, ELIZABETH. "Bibliography" [on women's traditional arts] Heresies no. 4, Winter 1978, pp. 124-5.
     Both feminist works and works describing women's traditional arts without feminist analysis are included in this listing of over 100 printed materials and films. The three main sections in which entries are grouped are Women's Art and Productive Work in Traditional Societies (divided by

continent), American Women's Traditional Work (with
separate sections for the social setting and for the crafts
themselves), and Developing a Feminist Art History.

218 Women as Artists and Women in the Arts: A Bibliography of Art
     Exhibition Catalogues Compiled from the Worldwide Art
     Catalogue Bulletin. Boston: Worldwide Books, 1978. 16 pp.
        "Compiled from the reviews in The Worldwide Art Catalogue
     Bulletin, this bibliography lists over 350 significant art
     catalogues from the past two decades. The selection consists
     primarily of monograph catalogues for one-man [sic] shows
     and group show catalogues which include the names of women
     artists in their titles, or which clearly imply the partici-
     pation of women artists.'' Exhibitions of anonymous crafts
     and folk art are excluded, but a few exhibitions based on
     women patrons or collectors are listed. Entries appear in
     the order in which they were published in the Bulletin;
     fortunately a name index is provided. Since artist, title
     of exhibition, name of gallery, city, and date are given in
     each case, this work has reference value in itself without
     consulting the periodical it indexes (which is actually a
     sort of glorified sales catalog for exhibition catalogs).

                              See also: 199, 329, 330, 331, 439, 480.

MUSIC

219 BLOCK, ADRIENNE FRIED and NEULS-BATES, CAROL. Women in American
     Music: A Bibliography of Music and Literature. Westport,
     Conn.: Greenwood Press, forthcoming.

220 BOWERS, JANE M. "Teaching about the History of Women in
     Western Music." Women's Studies Newsletter 5 (Summer
     1977):11-15.
        This description of a course on women in Western music
     from the Middle Ages to the present emphasizes their rela-
     tionship to the professional music world. The article
     incorporates the course's reading list, about 100 titles
     grouped by period, as well as a list of recordings used.

221 HIXON, DON L. and HENNESSEE, DON. Women in Music: A Biobib-
     liography. Metuchen, N.J.: Scarecrow Press, 1975. 347 pp.
        Over 4,000 classical musicians are listed in this work,
     more correctly titled an index than a biobibliography.
     Minimal biographical data (name with variants, dates, and
     field of musical activity) are provided for each woman,
     followed by a coded list of sources in which biographies
     may be found. These sources consist of forty-eight musical
     encyclopedias, dictionaries, or collective biographical
     works, most but not all in English, with imprints dated

from 1864 to 1974. There is no general index, but a classified list of women musicians makes it possible to locate women in any particular field.

222   POOL, JENNIE G. Women in Music History: A Research Guide. New York: the author, 1977. 42 pp. Available from Jennie G. Pool, P.O. Box 436, Ansonia Station, New York, N.Y. 10023.

This booklet contains not only a bibliography but also an essay on the history of women in music, a list of women composers born before 1900, and suggestions for research topics. The bibliography, although not extensive, is valuable because the author has tried not to duplicate other bibliographies but rather to list them in her own. Its contents include books and articles on women musicians in general and on individual women, approaches to women in history, bibliographies, lists of women composers, examples of denial of women's creative abilities in music, and other sources (periodicals, organizations, record companies.)

223   SKOWRONSKI, JoANN. Women in American Music: A Bibliography. Metuchen, N.J.: Scarecrow Prss, 1978. 183 pp.

Women from all fields of music from religious to pop during the period 1776-1976 are the subject of this annotated bibliography of 1305 books and articles. Some foreign-born musicians are also included if their contribution to American music was significant. The entries are grouped by period (1776-1834, 1835-1868, 1869-1938, 1939-1976), with added sections on general history and on bibliographies, dictionaries, and indexes. The name index lists persons mentioned in the annotations as well as those in the entries.

224   STERN, SUSAN. Women Composers: A Handbook. Metuchen, N.J.: Scarecrow Press, 1978. 191 pp.

This is an index to information on about 1,500 classical composers from the U.S., Canada, England, Belgium, France, West Germany, Austria, the Netherlands, Switzerland, and Italy, generally from the sixteenth century to the present, but including a few earlier composers for whom there is ample bibliography. The 260 sources indexed are chiefly in English, with a few French, German, Spanish, and Italian titles, ranging in date from the nineteenth century to the 1970s and in format from newspaper articles to multi-volume reference sets. The work also contains a list of several hundred composers for whom no data could be located and a supplementary bibliography of some sixty general references.

See also: 213.

PHILOSOPHY

225   BAZIN, NANCY TOPPING. "The Concept of Androgyny: A Working
       Bibliography." Women's Studies 2, no. 2 (1974):217-35.
       There are close to 200 annotated references in this
       interdisciplinary bibliography that covers the ground from
       Plato to present day feminism.

226   ENGLISH, JANE. "Review Essay: Philosophy." Signs 3 (Summer
       1978):823-31.
       This essay reviews recent work of feminist academic
       philosophers, citing in footnotes about eighty published
       and unpublished studies, largely dated from 1976 through
       early 1978. Topics considered include the relationship
       of feminism and philosophy, versions of androgynism, self-
       respect, abortion, and preferential hiring to eliminate sex
       discrimination.

227   MOULTON, JANICE. "Philosophy and Feminism: Recent Papers."
       Produced with the support of the Society for Women in
       Philosophy and the American Philosophical Association
       Committee on the Status of Women in the Profession. 1976.
       7 pp. Available from Janice Moulton, Dept. of Psychology,
       Duke University, Durham NC 27706.
       Nearly 150 journal articles, book chapters, and unpub-
       lished papers, mostly dated since 1974, are listed under
       the categories Abortion, Preferential Hiring and Equal
       Opportunity, Language, The Nature of Women, Relations
       between the Sexes, Women in the History of Philosophy, and
       The Women's Movement.

228   PIERCE, CHRISTINE. "Review Essay: Philosophy." Signs 1
       (Winter 1975):487-503.
       Philosophical research on sexism and feminism, chiefly
       between 1971 and 1975, is surveyed in this article. The
       subjects discussed include public policy (abortion and
       preferential hiring), political philosophy, conceptual
       analysis, analysis of language, feminist critiques of the
       history of philosophy and of contemporary philosophy, and
       the treatment of sexism and feminism in philosophy textbooks.
       There are about twenty-five titles cited in footnotes as
       well as a supplementary bibliography of sixty-five items.

229   WEBER, NANCY. Women in Philosophy, Twentieth Century: A
       Selectively Annotated Bibliography. Rohnert Park, Calif.:
       the author, 1978. 52 pp. Available from Nancy Weber,
       17101 Sonoma Highway, Sonoma, CA 95476.
       The main part of this bibliography lists the writings,
       philosophical and otherwise, of sixty-three twentieth-
       century women philosophers. The two appendixes present an

annotated bibliography of secondary sources on Harriet
Taylor Mill and a collection of seventy-two recent examples
of philosophical feminism by both women and men.

RELIGION

Bibliographies listing studies of religious attitudes towards abortion are listed with other bibliographies on abortion in the section
Health and Reproduction.

Christianity

Some of the bibliographies in this section contain a few references
concerned with other religions.

230   BASS, DOROTHY.   American Women in Church and Society, 1607-1920:
      A Bibliography.   Auburn Studies in Education, Publication
      no. 2.   New York: Union Theological Seminary, 1973.   37 pp.
         There is as much on society as on the church in this
      bibliography, although its stated focus is "the history of
      women in the American church, with an emphasis on Protest-
      antism."   Individual titles are generally not annotated,
      but the extensive notes at the beginning of subject sec-
      tions and occasional interspersed comments make it read
      almost like a bibliographic essay.

231   CERLING, C.E., Jr.   "An Annotated Bibliography of the New
      Testament Teaching about Women."   Journal of the Evangelical
      Theological Society 16 (1973):47-53.
         Citations to sixty-eight "works that show signs of serious
      scholarship and significant thought" dated from 1836 through
      1971, most of them in English, are arranged by author within
      three sections: books, periodical articles, theses.

232   DRIVER, ANNE BARSTOW.   "Review Essay: Religion."   Signs 2
      (Winter 1976):434-42.
         Writings critical of religious tradition as a cause of
      sexism are the subject of this survey.   Most of the seventy-
      plus books, articles, and papers listed in the footnotes are
      of Christian origin and were written between 1970 and 1976.

233   DUKE UNIVERSITY.   Divinity School Library.   Women in the Bible:
      A Bibliography.   Ed. Harriet V. Leonard.   Rev. and enl. ed.
      Durham, N.C.:   1977.   29 pp.
         Both women characters in the Bible and women as the
      subject of Biblical teaching are within the scope of this
      bibliography based on the library collection of a major

theological seminary. Citations are listed alphabetically within five sections: books in all languages, and articles in English, French, German, and other languages. Occasional brief annotations explain titles otherwise unclear, and there is a list of useful subject headings in the card catalog.

234   FARIANS, ELIZABETH. <u>Selected Bibliography on Women and Religion, 1965-1972</u>. 5th rev. ed. Cincinnati, Ohio: the author, 1973. 29 pp. Available from Elizabeth Farians, 6125 Webbland Pl., Cincinnati, Ohio, 54213.

    The majority of items cited in this bibliography are concerned with Christianity, but there are a few on Judaism. Its chronological arrangement (books are listed as before or after 1965, articles are listed by year) and the inclusion of many articles from popular and denominational magazines give it special value as a history of attitudes towards women in the church.

*235   FISCHER, CLARE B. <u>Breakthrough: Women in Theological Perspective</u>. Berkeley, Calif.: Center for Women in Religion and Library, Graduate Theological Union, forthcoming. Available from Center for Women in Religion, Graduate Theological Union, 2465 LeConte, Berkeley, CA 94709.

    The editor writes that this is planned to be a continuing bibliography issued quarterly, the first unit to contain approximately 125 pages and to consist of four sections: literature review, traditional approaches, women as research subjects and scholars, feminist approaches and selected periodical articles. It will list only works in English and reflect materials published in recent decades.

236   _____ and GATLIN, ROCHELLE. <u>Woman: A Theological Perspective: Bibliography and Addendum</u>. Berkeley, Calif.: Office of Women's Affairs, Graduate Theological Union, 1975. 70 pp. For address <u>see</u> 235.

    Created to promote the inclusion of information on women in the curriculum of a theological seminary, this topically arranged bibliography is most useful not for its sections on women's history, psychology, or socialization but rather for those on specifically religious topics: women and scriptures (both Old and New Testaments), women and theology, women in religion and society. Aside from one section on religion and cross-cultural studies, most of the books and articles dealing with religion are concerned with Christianity, Catholic and Protestant.

237   GANGHOFER, ODILE. The Woman in the Church: International
       Bibliography 1973-June 1975 Indexed by Computer/La Femme
       dans l'église: Bibliographie internationale 1973-juin 1975
       établie par ordinateur. RIC Supplement 21. Strasbourg
       Cedex, France: Cerdic Publications, 1975. 45 pp. Avail-
       able from Cerdic Publications, 9, Place de l'Université,
       F-67084 Strasbourg-Cedex, France.
           The Université des Sciences Humaines de Strasbourg
       sponsored the series of bibliographies from which this
       comes. Although English is the language most often seen
       among its entries, the chief value of the work lies in its
       "international and multiconfessional" inclusion of books
       and articles from European countries. (Titles in Greek or
       the Cyrillac alphabet are romanized and provided with a
       translation into French.) The 688 citations are grouped
       in broad subject categories: Woman, Church, and Society;
       Woman in the Church; Woman and the Ministries (i.e., as
       members of religious orders, ministers' wives, or mission-
       aries); Ordination of Women.

238   KENDALL, PATRICIA A. Women and the Priesthood: A Selected and
       Annotated Bibliography. Philadelphia: Committee to Promote
       the Cause of and to Plan for the Ordination of Women to the
       Priesthood, Episcopal Diocese of Pennsylvania, 1976. 57 pp.
           This bibliography is made up of 137 citations to books,
       articles, study reports, and tape cassettes selected to
       promote the ordination of women and intended for the use
       of the laity. Items included are chiefly readily accessible
       materials recently published in the U.S. and represent
       Roman Catholic and Protestant as well as Episcopal sources.
       In many cases the annotations amount to substantial
       abstracts, an especially useful feature in the case of the
       study reports.

239   KING, MARGOT. A Bibliography on Women and the Church. Sas-
       katoon, Sask.: Shannon Library, St. Thomas More College,
       1975. 66 pp.
           The compiler describes this bibliography as "complete
       as possible from 1970 to 1974 with the exception of news
       items and material of an ephemeral nature." About 1,000
       entries are divided into separate alphabetical sections in
       English (five-sixths of the total) and foreign languages
       (Dutch, French, German, Italian, Latin, Russian, Spanish),
       followed by lists of films and filmstrips, hymnals, news-
       letters, and packets or kits. Books and articles cited
       include both Catholic and Protestant publications as well
       as some articles from general periodicals, and despite the
       title there are a fair number of references to women in
       Judaism. There are no annotations, but more important
       items are starred.

240 PATRICK, ANNE E. "Women and Religion: A Survey of Significant Literature, 1965-1974." Theological Studies 36 (Dec. 1975):737-65. Reprinted, updated to 1975, in Woman: New Dimensions. Ed. Walter J. Burghardt. New York: Paulist Press, 1977, pp. 161-89.

The focus of this literature review is almost exclusively on Christianity, especially Roman Catholicism. It considers about 100 books and articles dealing with theological issues raised by the women's movement or with its effects on religious institutions. Topics covered include general and historical analyses and specific issues such as church law, liturgy, ministry, ordination, and models for Christian life.

241 "Selected Bibliography: Women, Language, and Theology." In The Power of Language Among the People of God: Report Received by the 191st General Assembly (1979) of the United Presbyterian Church, U.S.A. Forthcoming. Available from Advisory Council on Discipleship and Worship, 475 Riverside Drive, Room 1020, New York, N.Y. 10027.

Approximately 200 books, articles, and papers from scholarly, religious, and feminist sources are cited in this annotated bibliography. Most of them were published after 1970. The work is organized by subject, moving from broad general sections such as Women: History and Roles, or Language and Theology to narrower topics such as Language, Women, and the Church. One noteworthy section lists several sets of guidelines for nonsexist language in both religious and secular use.

242 WILSON, MARTHA M. "Women and Religion: Potential for Participation." Women Studies Abstracts 2 (Spring 1973):1-5.

243 _____ and WHALEY, SARA S. "Bibliography." Women Studies Abstracts 2 (Spring 1973):5-6, 92-94.

The article is a survey of the activities of women's groups within both the academic study of religion and Christian denominations, including bibliographic references to outstanding publications. It is followed by a listing, arranged by format, of some 100 special issues of periodicals, newsletters, bibliographies, books, and articles appearing between 1970 and 1973. Citations to books include references to their reviews other than those previously indexed in Women Studies Abstracts.

See also 160.

Judaism

244 BAUM, CHARLOTTE; HYMAN, PAULA; and MICHEL, SONYA. "Bibliography." In The Jewish Woman in America. New York: Dial Press, 1976, pp. 263-81.

Over 300 references are arranged by format: Memoirs and Autobiographies; Printed Primary Sources; Newspapers and Magazines; Archival Sources; Interviews; Fiction, Drama, Poetry; Secondary Sources. Some of the materials listed are too general to be useful to anyone engaged in research on the Jewish woman.

245   CANTOR, AVIVA. A Bibliography on the Jewish Woman: A Comprehensive and Annotated Listing of Works Published 1900-1978. Fresh Meadows, N.Y.: Biblio Press, 1979. 58 pp. Available from Biblio Press, P.O. Box 22, Fresh Meadows, N.Y. 11365.
      Despite its subtitle, this is a selected list of readily available books, articles, and papers providing basic information about Jewish women and about "the views of the educated or ignorant opposition." The annotations are both descriptive and evaluative: works considered characteristic of the opposition are tagged "Know the enemy." Topical chapters cover such subjects as history, religious life and law, Jewish women in the U.S., Canada, Israel, and other countries, and the Holocaust and resistance. Most of these chapters contain a section of fiction, and there are separate chapters for poetry and children's books. Many of the articles listed are from Jewish periodicals, and directories of Jewish publications and organizations and of feminist and other small presses are provided.

246   SCHLESINGER, BENJAMIN. The Jewish Family: A Survey and Annotated Bibliography. Toronto: University of Toronto Press, 1971. 175 pp.
      Introductory survey articles on the history of the Jewish family from biblical times to the shtetl of East Europe, Jewish families and intermarriage in the U.S., and family life in the kibbutz precede the 429-item bibliography of published materials in English. Topics covered in its subject arrangement include home, marriage, intermarriage, sexuality, health and welfare, death and mourning, divorce, the Holocaust, and the kibbutz, as well as geographical and period divisions. Three appendixes list 172 works of fiction dealing with Jewish life, statistical tables covering world Jewish population in 1968, and publishers' addresses.

See also: 239.

Other Religions

Most of the bibliographies listed in the geographical section on the Middle East contain materials on women in Islam.

247   LAYISH, AHARON. "Sources and Bibliography." In his Women and Islamic Law in a Non-Moslem State: A Study Based on Decisions of the Shari'a Courts in Israel. Shiloah Center for

Middle Eastern and African Studies, Tel Aviv University.
Studies in Islamic Culture and History. New York: J. Wiley,
1975, pp. 339-50.
   The sources cited include archival material, Islamic
legal collections and commentaries, official and statistical
publications, newspapers and periodicals, and about eighty
books, articles, and unpublished dissertations.

248   YOUNG, KATHERINE K. and SHARMA, ARVIND. Images of the Feminine,
      Mythic, Philosophic and Human, in the Buddhist, Hindu, and
      Islamic Traditions: A Bibliography of Women in India.
      Chico, Calif.: New Horizons Press, 1974. 36 pp. Available
      from New Horizons Press, P.O. Box 1758, Chico, CA 95926.
         "This bibliography was initiated at Harvard's Center for
      the Study of World Religions in response to requests by
      students and research associates at Harvard Divinity School
      working in the domain of women in religion." It also,
      however, contains titles on mythology, philosophy, the
      arts, and politics. More than 400 books, scholarly articles,
      conference papers, unpublished manuscripts, and government
      documents from the nineteenth century to the early 1970s
      are listed. Most are in English, but some are in Hindi,
      and the many titles published in India constitute the
      chief value of the work.

EDUCATION

Bibliographies on topics related to education are to be found in a
number of other sections as well as this one. Studies of sex bias in
textbooks are listed in several of the titles in the section Children's
Literature and Textbooks. Under Economics, bibliographies on women
as educators are listed among Specific Occupations, those on vocational
education in the section Vocational Guidance, and those on continuing
education in the section Employment Reentry. Achievement Motivation,
Language and Nonverbal Communication, and Mathematics Learning are all
sections under Psychology.

General

249   "Access of Women to Education." Bulletin of the International
      Bureau of Education 174 (1970):18-105.

250   CISMARESCO, FRANÇOISE. "Education and Training of Women."
      Educational Documentation and Information 196 (1975):14-46.
         This update of "Access of Women to Education" (249)
      covers publications for the years 1970-1975 and includes
      materials on vocational training as well as on academic

education. Most of the 233 citations to books, journal
articles, and government and international documents are
annotated. Titles of those not in English or French are
translated into English. The arrangement is geographical
(general works, Africa, Latin America, North America, Asia,
Eastern Europe, Western Europe, Oceania) with an author
index.

251 HARRIS, ABIGAIL M. ETS Studies Related to Women and Education:
Annotated Bibliography. Research Memorandum RM 76-8.
Princeton, N.J.: Educational Testing Service, 1976. 93
pp. Available from EDRS, ED 138 603.
  Although Educational Testing Service was responsible for
the research represented in this bibliography, the 153
studies listed were issued in a variety of forms, including
books, journal articles, and government documents as well
as ETS publications. Some of them are confidential and not
to be used without the author's permission. The entries,
each with a lengthy summary, are arranged in four categories:
research primarily about women, studies focused on sex differences and similarities, studies in which data by sex are
provided but the focus is not on sex differences, and methods
of determining and correcting for bias and/or differences.
There is an author index.

252 NATIONAL FOUNDATION FOR THE IMPROVEMENT OF EDUCATION. Resource
Center on Sex Roles in Education. Title IX: Se-
lected Resources. Washington: Dept. of Health, Education,
and Welfare, Education Division, Office of Education; for
sale by Supt. of Docs., U.S. Govt. Print. Off., 1977. 5,
A-5 pp.
  The texts of the Title IX Regulation, with explanatory
comments, and of a related Office of Civil Rights memorandum
on athletics introduce this bibliography. There follow an
annotated list of twenty-five general resources (articles,
reports, pamphlets) and an appendix citing guidelines,
policy statements, and directories issued by sixteen states.

253 "Sources Of Information On Women's Education" and "Select
Bibliography." International Review of Education 19, no.
1 (1973):172-80.
  This international listing of nongovernmental organizations, specialist libraries, bibliographies, and other
publications in English, French, and German excludes from
its 113-item bibliography all titles cited in Astin (296)
and in "Access of Women to Education: (249). Its value
lies in its coverage of writings from countries other than
the U.S.

254   Women's Educational Equity: Annotated Selected References
         and Resources. Bibliography Series, no. 1. San Francisco:
         Women's Educational Equity Communications Network, 1977.
         16 pp. Available from Far West Laboratory for Educational
         Research and Development, 1855 Folsom St., San Francisco,
         CA 94103.
               Intended as "an introductory overview of major resources,"
         this highly selective bibliography is arranged by format:
         Books/Reports/Bibliographies, Journals, Newsletters/Resource
         Publications, Library Collections. All publications are of
         very recent date, and the descriptive annotations include
         full order information where available.

*255   WOMEN'S EDUCATIONAL EQUITY COMMUNICATIONS NETWORK. Network
         News and Notes. San Francisco, 1977- Monthly. Available
               This newsletter regularly includes lists of publications
         on women's education and employment.

                                          See also: 007, 094, 405, 443, 485.

         History of Education

256   BURSTYN, JOAN N. "Women's Education in England during the
         Nineteenth Century: A Review of the Literature, 1970-1976."
         History of Education 6 (Feb. 1977):11-19.
               In addition to the nearly fifty recent books and scholarly
         articles listed alphabetically at the close of the essay,
         the author cites about half as many older works in footnotes.

257   SCHNORRENBERG, BARBARA BRANDON. "Education for Women in
         Eighteenth Century England: An Annotated Bibliography."
         Women and Literature 4 (Spring 1976):49-55.
               Only primary source materials are included in this bib-
         liography of twenty-seven items. The annotations describe
         each title at length.

                                                        See also: 423.

         Elementary and Secondary Education

258   LEVY, BETTY. "The School's Role in the Sex Role Stereotyping
         of Girls: A Feminist Review of the Literature." Feminist
         Studies 1 (Summer 1972):5-23.
               The eighty-six works cited at the close of this litera-
         ture review include "research studies, informal reports and
         speculative writings that bear on the school's role in
         elaborating and reinforcing damaging sex roles."

259   SHERIDAN, E. MARCIA. <u>Sex Differences and Reading: An Annotated Bibliography</u>. Newark, Del.: International Reading
Association, 1976. 40 pp. Available from International
Reading Association, 800 Barksdale Rd., P.O. Box 8139,
Newark, DE 19711.
        In an attempt to cover all studies on reading achieve-
ment in which sex is a major variable, this bibliography
annotates 154 titles, principally journal articles published since 1960. Most of them appear in the sections
concerned specifically with reading achievement, methods,
and materials. Other sections list studies seeking reasons
for sex differences in reading, such as sex of teacher,
separate sex classes, and different treatment of boys and
girls. The concluding sections deal more briefly with sex
differences in attitudes, achievement, and psychology and
with the development of sex roles.

260   VROEGH, KAREN. "Sex of Teacher and Academic Achievement: A
Review of Research." <u>Elementary School Journal</u> 76 (April
1976):389-405.
        The studies reviewed cover the period from 1908 through
1975 and include dissertations, monographs, and articles
from educational and psychological journals. Over 100
citations are listed alphabetically at the close of the
essay.

See also: 261, 265.

Higher Education

261   MUHICH, DOLORES. "Sex Discrimination Patterns in Higher Education." Unpublished paper for the American Association
for the Advancement of Science Social-Psychological Prize
Contest, 1974. 51 pp. Available from EDRS, ED 114 994.
        This literature review discusses the effects of cultural
conditioning, the attitude of high school counselors,
problems with college admissions and financial aid, and
employment conditions after earning one or more advanced
degrees. The accompanying list of about eighty references
includes published and unpublished materials, most of them
dated since 1970.

262   OLTMAN, RUTH M. <u>Status of Graduate and Professional Education
of Women--1974: A Review of the Literature and Bibliography</u>.
14 pp. Available from EDRS, ED 092 022.
        The sixty-eight recent titles listed in the bibliography
are described in the review essay under the headings:
Background and Current Developments, Social Factors
Attitudes, Institutional Barriers, Trends in Specific
Disciplines, Requirements of the Law, Proposed Solutions.

263 WESTERVELT, ESTHER MANNING. <u>Barriers to Women's Participation</u>
<u>in Postsecondary Education: A Review of Research and Com-</u>
<u>mentary as of 1973-74.</u> Washington: National Center for
Educational Statistics, for sale by Supt. of Docs., U.S.
Govt. Print. Off., 1975. 76 pp. Available from EDRS, ED
111 256.

The title page describes this as an expanded, updated,
and revised version of an original draft by Ruth B. Ekstrom.
The review was undertaken in preparation for a survey
program to determine the extent and causes of women's non-
participation in postsecondary education. It analyzes the
institutional barriers, social constraints, and psychological factors responsible. The 272-item bibliography that
completes the essay is more convenient to use than those
in most literature reviews because items are numbered and
are referred to by number in the text.

264 _____ and FIXTER, DEBORAH A. <u>Women's Higher and Continuing</u>
<u>Education: An Annotated Bibliography with Selected Refer-</u>
<u>ences on Related Aspects of Women's Lives.</u> New York:
College Entrance Examination Board, 1971. 67 pp.

The principal focus of this bibliography is on higher
and continuing education, with decreasing attention paid
to the related topics of employment, social roles, psychological development, and sex differences. Although the
work has now become dated, it is still valuable for its
selectivity (both significance and availability weighed
heavily among the criteria), its detailed subject organization, and its annotations. A variety of materials are
included; the largest number are journal articles, books,
and government documents.

See also: 297, 343, 431.

Women's Studies

While this entire book lists bibliographies <u>for</u> women's studies,
the section that follows lists bibliographies <u>about</u> women's
studies.

265 AHLUM, CAROL. <u>High School Feminist Studies.</u> Old Westbury,
N.Y.: Feminist Press, 1976. 157 pp.

Although this work is composed chiefly of reviews of
high school textbooks in U.S. history and English literature and syllabi for women's studies courses, it also
includes a bibliography of about fifty secondary sources.

266 "Resource Guide." <u>Canadian Newsletter of Research on Women</u> 6
(Supp. May 1977):140-41.

Its Canadian focus gives significance to this brief list of directories, reports, and conference proceedings used in compiling a guide to women's studies courses and their instructors in Canadian colleges and universities.

267 ROBINSON, LORA H. <u>Women's Studies: Courses and Programs for Higher Education</u>. Washington: American Association for Higher Education, 1973. 54 pp. Available from EDRS, ED 074 997.

A documented survey of courses and programs at a selected group of institutions is followed by a bibliography of over 100 reports, articles, pamphlets, and ERIC papers.

268 ZANGRANDO, JOANNA SCHNEIDER. "Women's Studies in the United States: Approaching Reality." <u>American Studies International</u> 14 (Autumn 1975):15-36. Reprinted in <u>American Studies: Topics and Sources</u>. Ed. Robert H. Walker. Westport, Conn.: Greenwood Press, 1976. pp. 238-57.

This bibliographic essay on "the development, within the past half-dozen years, of scholarly, academically-oriented Women's Studies courses, programs, research, resources and resource repositories, publications, and communications networks" is acquiring historical value as it loses timeliness.

ECONOMICS

This section includes bibliographies on women in any occupation, paid or unpaid.

General

269 KAHNE, HILDA. "Review Essay: Economic Research on Women and Families." <u>Signs</u> 3 (Spring 1978):652-65.

270 _____ and HYBELS, JUDITH. <u>Work and Family Issues: A Bibliography of Economic and Related Social Science Research</u>. Wellesley, Mass.: Wellesley Center for Research on Women in Higher Education and the Professions, 1978. 22 pp.

The literature review describes selected published and unpublished materials on women's employment and related family issues that appeared or were written between mid-1975 and December 1976. Although it emphasizes economics, it includes the writings of other social scientists as well as economists. Citations appear only in the thirty-five footnotes, but all of them are also listed in the separate bibliography by Kahne and Hybels. This compilation of close to 300 entries covers research for the same period more comprehensively but without commentary on individual items. Its topical organization takes up both paid and nonmarket work as well as family issues, migration, and life cycle issues.

271   _____ and KOHEN, ANDREW I. "Economic Perspectives on the Roles of Women in the American Economy." Journal of Economic Literature 13 (December 1975):1249-92.
       The American Economics Association Committee on the Status of Women in the Economics Profession suggested the preparation of this literature review that seeks to present in nontechnical language a survey of recent economic literature on women, identifying topics in which economists are interested, and describing some of their findings. Primary emphasis is on women's economic roles in the labor market and in the household, including a section on the relation of women's changing role to social policy. The accompanying bibliography has 267 entries.

272   KOHEN, ANDREW I.; BREINICH, SUSAN G.; and SHIELDS, PATRICIA. Women and the Economy: A Bibliography and a Review of the Literature on Sex Differentiation in the Labor Market. Columbus: Center for Human Resource Research, Ohio State University, 1977. 109 pp.
       This attempt at a comprehensive listing of research on women as workers is confined almost entirely to recent studies having to do with the U.S. Purely descriptive works and those having to do with education and vocational choice are excluded. About 600 titles (books, articles, dissertations, technical reports) are listed under twenty-seven categories that include labor supply, earnings, specific occupations, unemployment, unions, law, home production, and child care. The literature review concludes with a table summarizing research on sex differentials in earnings. (A 1975 edition of this work, identical in all respects except for a twenty-page supplement adding about 100 titles to the bibliography, is available from NTIS, PB 241 193 and from EDRS, ED 112 099).

Housework

273   FELMLEY, JENROSE. Working Women: Homemakers and Volunteers: An Annotated Selected Bibliography. Washington: Business and Professional Women's Federation, 1975. 25 pp.
       In this title "working" for once does not mean "gainfully employed." A review of the literature on "the issues, problems, and recommendations surrounding the occupation of homemaker" is followed by an annotated bibliography of eighty-two representative publications from scholarly, popular, and feminist sources, chiefly published between 1970 and 1975.

274   GLAZER–MALBIN, NONA. "Review Essay: Housework." Signs 1
      (Summer 1976):905-22.
      This article reviews research from the mid-1950s through
      1975 on housework as a division of labor and from 1970
      through 1975 on the monetary value of housework, the social
      role of the housewife, and housework and the political
      economy. Over sixty titles, including several studies then
      in progress, are cited in the footnotes.

Volunteer Work

275   GOLD, DORIS B. Opposition to Volunteerism: An Annotated Bib-
      liography. CPL Bibliography no. 8. Chicago: Council of
      Planning Librarians, 1979. 21 pp.
      Focus of this bibliography is on feminist opposition to
      service volunteerism in the 1970s, and materials on other
      kinds of volunteer opposition, such as army service, are
      excluded. The work is organized into four main categories:
      Bibliographies, Background, General, and Economic Aspects.
      Within each of these, entries are divided by type of material
      (books, periodical and newspaper articles, reports, etc.),
      and the general section contains a noteworthy listing of
      NOW bulletins and reports on the subject.

276   RUTGERS UNIVERSITY. Center for the American Woman and Politics.
      Voluntary Participation among Women in the United States:
      A Selected Bibliography, 1950-1976. New Brunswick, N.J.:
      the Center, 1976. 35 pp.
      "The bibliography contains citations to published, un-
      published, and ongoing work regarding the political, social,
      psychological, or economic character of the voluntary parti-
      cipation of women in the United States. . . .Studies
      concerning the ideology, motivations, and rewards of women's
      volunteerism are also included." Although a large propor-
      tion of the references have to do with political activity,
      other forms of volunteerism are represented. Both scholarly
      and popular writings with dates between 1950 and June 1976
      are listed in sections by format: Bibliographies; Directo-
      ries and Encyclopedias; Periodicals; Books, Monographs, and
      Reports; Articles; Dissertations and Unpublished Papers;
      Research in Progress. There is an author index.

277   SMITH, CONSTANCE and FREEDMAN, ANNE. Voluntary Associations:
      Perspectives on the Literature. Cambridge: Harvard Uni-
      versity Press, 1972. 250 pp.
      Although this extensive literature review is the out-
      growth of Smith's concern with the role of educated women
      in modern society, it deals with volunteerism on the part
      of both women and men. The work is organized into eight

topical chapters, each concluding with a bibliography that lists both the titles discussed in that chapter (unannotated) and a number of others related to its subject (with annotations). Most of the bibliographies have at least 100 entries, with little duplication of titles. Writings cited are predominantly scholarly academic literature; materials produced by voluntary organizations for their membership are excluded. There is an author index.

See also: 273.

Employment

278 BAYEFSKY, EVELYN. "Women and Work: A Selection of Books and Articles." Ontario Library Review 56 (June 1972):79-90.
Although now outdated in most respects, this annotated bibliography of over 100 books, articles, and government documents is still useful for its coverage of Canadian materials.

279 BICKNER, MEI LIANG. Women at Work: An Annotated Bibliography. Los Angeles: Manpower Research Center, Institute of Industrial Relations, University of California, 1974? [unpaginated] Available from EDRS, ED 095 398.

280 _____ and SHAUGHNESSY, MARLENE. Women at Work, Volume 2: An Annotated Bibliography, 1973-1975. Los Angeles: Institute of Industrial Relations, University of California, 1977. [unpaginated]
The issue of working women is viewed primarily from an economic and social perspective in these compilations, each of which contains about 600 references to scholarly studies, government documents, and report literature. The first covers the period from 1960 through summer 1973; the second extends the coverage through 1975. With the exception of a few especially significant titles, works listed are concerned with working women in the U.S. only. Special effort was made to include writings on nonprofessional and minority women and on legal developments. Generous means of access are provided by the classified arrangement and the author, title, cross reference, and keyword indexes. In addition, the second volume offers an annotated list of the indexes and abstracting services that the compilers found most useful.

281 CATALYST. Library. Bibliographies. New York: 1975-1978. Available from Catalyst, 14 E. 60th St., New York, N.Y. 10022.
Catalyst, a nonprofit organization offering counseling and employment services to women through a national network of resource centers, also issues a number of publications,

including this series of over thirty bibliographies on aspects of women's employment in general or in specific occupations. (A price list is available on request.) They vary in length from a dozen to nearly 100 titles, citing popular and social science literature, government documents, newspaper articles, and unpublished papers. All materials listed in current bibliographies are available for consultation in the library of their National Headquarters or may be ordered in photocopy.

282   FRANK, GENEVIÈVE. Women at Work and in Society: A Selected Bibliography 1970-1975/La Femme au Travail et dans la Societé: Bibliographie Sélective, 1970-1975. Geneva: International Institute for Labour Studies, 1975? 44 pp. Available from International Institute for Labour Studies, Case postale 6, 1211 Geneva 22, Switzerland.
       Broad international coverage distinguishes this bibliography prepared for an International Woman's Year symposium on women and decision-making. It lists over 500 books and articles in English and French published from 1970 through 1975. The principal emphasis is on women and work, and the largest category in its subject arrangement, that on women's participation in the labor force, is subdivided to provide for studies dealing with individual countries and occupations. Other topics considered include women's motivation, education, and roles in the economy and society, division of labor between sexes, and the relation of work to family. There is an author index.

*283   International Bibliography of Economics/Bibliographie international de science économique. vol.1- London: Tavistock Publications; Chicago: Aldine Publishing Co., 1952- Annual.
       Section G2242, titled Organization of Production: Women, constitutes an international continuing bibliography on employment of women.

284   KIEVIT, MARY BACH. Review and Synthesis of Research on Women in the World of Work. Information Series, no. 56. Columbus: ERIC Clearinghouse on Vocational and Technical Education, Ohio State University; for sale by Supt. of Docs., U.S. Govt. Print. Off., 1972. 96 pp. Available from EDRS, ED 066 553.
       The literature of both business and education was searched for the period 1968-1971 to prepare this review of research on women's employment in the U.S. and abroad. Although the concluding list of about 200 references is now dated, the analysis and comment are still valuable and are made especially accessible by the inclusion with each citation of the page number on which the work is discussed.

285   NIEVA, VERONICA F. and GUTEK, BARBARA A. "Women and Work: A
      Bibliography of Psychological Research." Catalog of
      Selected Documents in Psychology 6 (May 1976):50. MS 1257.
      16 pp.
          This list of 217 references concerned with the psychology
      of women and paid work outside the home consists chiefly of
      articles from 62 journals in the social and behavioral
      sciences, business, women's studies, and the popular press,
      but it also includes some unpublished papers, dissertations,
      and chapters from books. 70 percent of the titles appeared
      in the 1970s. Arrangement is alphabetical without subject
      index or annotations, but each entry is coded by content,
      level of analysis, and type of article.

286   ORGANIZATION FOR ECONOMIC COOPERATION AND DEVELOPMENT. Library.
      Le travail des femmes/Women's Labor. Bibliographie spéciale
      analytique/Special Annotated Bibliography. Paris: The
      Organization, 1976. 161 pp.

*287 U.S CIVIL SERVICE COMMISSION. Library. Equal Opportunity in
      Employment. Personnel Bibliography Series, nos. 38, 49,
      65, 72, 88, 95. Washington: U.S. Govt. Print. Off., 1971,
      1973, 1975-78.
          These bibliographies are more-or-less annual acquisition
      lists of books, periodical articles, and dissertations
      added to the Civil Service Commission Library. (Materials
      added between editions are listed in the Library's monthly
      publication, Personnel Literature.) Each bibliography
      contains a substantial section of twenty pages or more on
      employment of women divided into the categories General
      Aspects; Executive, Managerial and Professional Postions;
      and Women in Federal, State, and Local Governments. There
      are only occasional annotations, but the set of descriptors
      supplied for each title gives an idea of its scope.

288   U.S. WOMEN'S BUREAU. A Guide to Sources of Data on Women and
      Women Workers for the United States and for Regions, States,
      and Local Areas. Washington: U.S. Govt. Print. Off.,
      1972. 15 pp.
          "This listing identifies selected [government] publica-
      tions currently available or soon to be published on persons
      by sex, race, educational attainment, labor force participa-
      tion, occupation, and industry." Within its subject arrange-
      ment publications are grouped by issuing agency, with
      contents and geographical coverage indicated.

289   WARD, DENNIS. Sex Discrimination in Employment, 1969-1975:
      A Selective Bibliography. Part 1. Cases and Comments.
      Sacramento: California State Law Library, 1976. 15 pp.

This work consists of notes and comments on thirty-one
leading Federal and California court decisions from 1969
through the period indexed in the October 1975 issue of
Index to Legal Periodicals. Although one may encounter
references elsewhere to a second part covering periodical
articles, this was never published and is no longer planned.

*290   Women at Work: An ILO Newsbulletin. Geneva: Office for Women
       Workers' Questions, International Labour Office. 1977-
       Semi-annual.
            Since 1978 each issue has carried a bibliography of books,
       articles, and international documents on a chosen topic.
       Topics covered in 1978 were Women Workers in Rural Areas,
       1975-1978 and Women in Non-Traditional Occupations, 1976-
       1978.

                                        *See also: 002, *255, 437, 484.*

Labor History

291   American Women; Our Lives and Labor: An Annotated Bibliography
       on Women and Work in the United States, 1900-1975. Eugene,
       Oreg.: Feminist Theory Collective, 1976. 36 pp. Available
       from Amazon Reality, P.O. Box 95, Eugene OR 97401.
            Criteria for inclusion in this highly selective bibliog-
       raphy were readability, availability, representation of
       Third World women and houseworkers, and descriptive rather
       than theoretical qualities. The annotations reflect the
       attitudes of the socialist and feminist study group that
       produced the work and are the reason for its inclusion here.

*292   "Annual Bibliography On American Labor History." Labor History
       (Fall issue)
            Beginning with the bibliography for 1976 (which appeared
       in vol. 18, 1977) this has contained sections on women or
       women and children within each of its period divisions.

293   BULKLEY, CONSTANCE. Women and Work: A Preliminary Guide to
       Primary Sources in the Labor-Management Documentation Center.
       Ithaca, N.Y.: Labor-Management Documentation Center, Martin
       P. Catherwood Library, New York School of Industrial and
       Labor Relations, Cornell University, 1975. 17 pp.
            "This is a preliminary guide to collections in the Center
       in which women were either directly involved as workers,
       labor leaders, or arbitrators, or indirectly as women
       prominent in the administration of relevant voluntary
       organizations." The first part consists of the descriptions
       of 19 manuscript collections, the second of an unannotated
       listing of about 150 pamphlets in a collection that goes
       back as far as the early twentieth century.

294   INTERNATIONAL LABOUR OFFICE. Central Library and Documenta-
       tion Branch. Bibliography on Women Workers/Bibliographie
       sur le travail des femmes (1861-1965) [comp. by Suzanne
       Nicolas]. Bibliographical Contributions, no. 26. Geneva:
       International Labour Office, 1970. 252 pp.
       Broad international coverage (the index lists over 100
       countries or regions) marks this bibliography. Within its
       eleven subject chapters items are listed chronologically,
       giving a historical overview. They include books, articles,
       reports, and an outstanding number of government and inter-
       national documents. There are four indexes: personal
       authors, corporate authors (other than ILO), subjects, and
       geographical areas.

295   SOLTOW, MARTHA JANE, and WERY, MARY K. American Women and the
       Labor Movement, 1825-1974: An Annotated Bibliography.
       Metuchen, N.J.: Scarecrow Press, 1976. 247 pp.
       Abstracts are supplied for nearly all the 700-plus
       citations to books, articles, pamphlets, and U.S. govern-
       ment publications in this work. (Most dissertations and
       state government documents are excluded.) Arrangement is
       by subject categories, several of them subdivided: employ-
       ment, trade unions, working conditions, strikes, legisla-
       tion, worker education, labor leaders, supportive efforts.
       There are author, subject, and cross-reference indexes and
       an appendix listing U.S. archives holding material related
       to women and labor.

Vocational Guidance

This section lists bibliographies concerned primarily with women's
choice of occupation, career counseling, and vocational education.

296   ASTIN, HELEN S.; SUNIEWICK, NANCY; and DWECK, SUSAN. Women:
       A Bibliography on Their Education and Careers. New York:
       Behavioral Publications, 1974. 243 pp.
       The 352 studies cited in this bibliography (originally
       published in 1971) are principally empirical research done
       in the 1960s, and the long abstract supplied for each title
       describes both its conclusions and its methods. Organiza-
       tion is by subject categories which include determinants
       of career choice, marital and family adjustment of working
       women, women in the world of work, sex roles and socializa-
       tion, historical and economic accounts, policy studies,
       and continuing education. Introductory essays give an
       overview and interpretations of the various findings, and
       there are author and subject indexes.

297   BARRABAS, JEAN.   Women; Their Educational and Career Roles:
      An Annotated Bibliography.   ERIC-IRCD Urban Disadvantaged
      Series, no. 31.   New York: Columbia University, ERIC
      Clearinghouse on the Urban Disadvantaged, 1972.   71 pp.
      Available from EDRS, ED 067 423.
         This work is made up of brief abstracts for ERIC docu-
      ments listed in Research in Education from November 1966
      through December 1971 and journal articles listed in
      Current Index to Journals in Education from January 1969
      through December 1971.   Much of the literature is research
      oriented.   It is organized into sections that include
      counseling women, women as students, continuing education,
      career choice, and women in the world of work.

298   Career Counseling; New Perspectives for Women and Girls:
      Selected Annotated Bibliography.   Washington: Business
      and Professional Women's Foundation, 1972.   44 pp.
         The greater part of this slim bibliography describes
      research materials on counseling and occupational choice.
      The last quarter is concerned with resources on locating
      and getting jobs in specific careers.

299   HARWAY, MICHELE, et al.   Sex Discrimination in Guidance and
      Counseling: Annotations.   Los Angeles: Higher Education
      Research Institute, 1976.   177 pp.   Available from EDRS,
      ED 132 500.
         This abstract bibliography lists 167 items, all published
      since 1970 except for a few classic references from the
      sixties.   The entries include books, journal articles, and
      research reports covering a wide range of topics related
      to sex discrimination in counseling and in education in
      general.   The work is alphabetically arranged without index
      or other subject approach.

300   Nonsexist Career Counseling: Annotated Selected References
      and Resources.   Parts 1-2.   Bibliography Series, no. 3.
      San Francisco: Women's Educational Equity Communications
      Network, 1978.   23, 29 pp.   Available from Far West Labor-
      atory for Educational Research and Development, 1855 Folsom
      St., San Francisco, CA 94103.
         The first part of this bibliography lists publications
      (books, articles, research reports, government and ERIC
      documents) on the training and development of career
      counselors for women, nonsexist career counseling, measure-
      ment of women's career interest, and career counseling for
      minority women.   Part 2 cites similar publications on women
      and work and women in specific occupations or professions
      and describes more than fifty programs related to women's
      career preparation, curriculum materials development, and
      staff training.

301 PHELPS, ANN T.; FARMER, HELEN S.; and BACKER, THOMAS E. Selected
    Annotated Bibliography on Women at Work. Los Angeles:
    Human Interaction Research Institute, 1975. 102 pp.
    Available from EDRS, ED 127 520.

302 _____. New Career Options for Women: A Selected Annotated
    Bibliography. New York: Human Sciences Press, 1977.
    144 pp.
    The bibliographic content of these two works is identical
    except for section titles and slight variations in arrange-
    ment. Both versions contain the same 240 abstracts for
    research studies, theoretical papers, and literature reviews
    selected to accompany a sourcebook for vocational counselors.
    Most of the titles were published after 1970. Topics covered
    include career opportunities for women, their legal rights
    in regard to work, counseling techniques, and such special
    issues as maternal employment, sex differences, and achieve-
    ment motivation. Author and subject indexes appear only in
    the commercially published version.

303 STAKELON, ANNE E. and MAGISOS, JOEL H. Sex Stereotyping and
    Occupational Aspiration: An Annotated Bibliography. Biblio-
    graphy Series, no. 29. Columbus: Ohio State University,
    Center for Vocational Education, 1975. 49 pp. Available
    from EDRS, ED 118 926.
    "Prepared to assist those applying for grants under Part D
    of the Vocational Education Act of 1963" by informing them
    about previous and current research, this bibliography lists
    eighty-eight citations to journal articles or report literature.
    They are grouped into sections according to the data base from
    which they were retrieved: Abstracts of Instructional and Re-
    search Materials in Vocational and Technical Education, Resources
    in Education, and Current Index to Journals in Education.

See also: 250.

Employment Reentry

See also Middle Age Women.

304 Continuing Education: Reentry and the Mature Woman, Annotated
    References and Resources. Bibliography Series, no. 2. San
    Francisco: Women's Educational Equity Communications
    Network, 1977. 20 pp. Available from Far West Laboratory
    for Educational Research and Development, 1855 Folsom St.,
    San Francisco, CA 94103.
    The references cited consist of eighty-five books,
    articles, reports, government publications, and ERIC docu-
    ments. All are currently available and full order informa-
    tion is given. The works are listed topically under the

headings Overviews and Bibliographies, The Mature Woman
Student, Counseling Resources, Program Development, and
Specific Programs. Descriptions of eight Women's Educational Equity Act projects for reentry women complete the
bibliography.

305   TITTLE, CAROL KEHR and DENKER, ELENOR RUBIN. "Re-Entry Women:
      A Selective Review of the Educational Process, Career Choice,
      and Interest Measurement." Review of Educational Research
      47 (Fall 1977):531-84.
      Topics considered in this literature review include
      barriers and opportunities for mature women in post-
      secondary education, theory and research on career choice
      for women, especially reentry women, and sex bias in
      interest measurement. The works discussed appear at the
      close as a list of more than 150 references.

See also: 264, 297.

Child Care and Maternal Employment

*306   Day Care. Subject Bibliography SB-092. Washington: U.S.
       Govt. Print. Off. Annual?
       This partially annotated price list of U.S. government
       publications includes only those in print at the time of
       issue. The bibliography dated August 28, 1978 listed about
       thirty titles.

307   Family Day Care: An Annotated Bibliography. Project Child
      Care Paper no. 1. Toronto: Community Day Care Coalition
      and the Social Planning Council of Metropolitan Toronto,
      1975. 38 pp. Available from EDRS, ED 119 875.
      Family day care is defined here as a woman caring for
      one or more children in her own home, especially if she
      cares for her own children at the same time. The seventy
      titles described are recent Canadian and U.S. publications
      which focus on the issues of the quality of family day
      care and the support systems called for. Although they are
      alphabetically arranged, an appendix lists those concerned
      with each of these issues. Additional appendixes give
      sources for audiovisual materials, contact persons in
      Ontario, and other bibliographies on day care.

308   HOWARD, NORMA KEMEN. Day Care: An Abstract Bibliography.
      Urbana, Ill.: ERIC Clearinghouse on Early Childhood Educa-
      tion, 1971. 19 pp. Available from EDRS, ED 052 823.

309   _____. _____. Supp. 1, 1972. 59 pp. Available from EDRS,
      ED 069 402.

310 _____. _____. Supp. 2, 1974. 60 pp. Available from EDRS,
ED 089 884.
    The terms "Day Care Programs" and "Day Care Services"
were used for the search of the ERIC data bases <u>Research
in Education</u> and <u>Current Index to Journals in Education</u>
that produced this series of bibliographies. The three
parts together cover publications indexed from the beginning
of 1970 through early 1974, a total of nearly 300 research
reports, conference papers, pamphlets, and journal articles.
Each part consists of an alphabetical list of ERIC documents
and another of journal articles, without subject access.
Only the ERIC documents have abstracts.

311 HU, TEH-WEI. <u>Selected Bibliography on Child Care Evaluation
Studies</u>. Exchange Bibliography 440. Monticello, Ill.:
Council of Planning Librarians, 1973. 9 pp.
    Over 100 references to books, articles, and government
documents from the 1960s and 1970s are listed alphabetically
within three sections: Conceptual Issues; Costs; and Bene-
fits (Effectiveness).

312 LLOYD, DIANE. <u>Child Care in the 1970's: A Bibliography</u>.
Exchange Bibliography 1216-1217. Monticello, Ill.: Council
of Planning Librarians, 1977. 97 pp.
    This work is the result of a literature search for
"empirical research and evaluation studies on the effects
of day care." Citations to over 1,200 publications with
an imprint date of January 1, 1970 or later are organized
in a classified arrangement that includes a section on day
care in countries other than the U.S.

313 SALO, KRISTINE O. "Maternal Employment and Children's Behavior:
A Review of the Literature." <u>Catalog of Selected Documents
in Psychology</u> 5 (Summer 1975):277. MS 1007. 30 pp.
    This paper surveys the literature on effects of mother's
employment on children's personality and behavior. The
author points out recurring research problems, recommends
improved methods, and suggests the possibility that changing
social attitudes may produce different results from future
research. A list of thirty-two references cites books and
journal articles from the behavioral sciences dated from
1948 through 1973.

314 SEEGMILLER, BONNI R. "Maternal Employment: A Bibliography."
<u>Catalog of Selected Documents in Psychology</u> 5 (Spring 1975):
233. MS 927. 27 pp.
    This is an alphabetical compilation of 282 references to
books, theses, dissertations, documents, and reports gleaned
from other lists of references and from searches of <u>Child
Development Abstracts</u> and <u>Psychological Abstracts</u> as far

back as the 1930s. The author's abstract, which defines
the trends in this literature and the types of further
research needed, is the only commentary.

Part-time Employment and Job Sharing

315   Alternative Work Patterns: General References. Bibliography
      P1A. New York: Catalyst, 1977. 6 pp.

316   _____: Job Sharing/Paired Employment. Bibliography P1B.
      New York: Catalyst, 1977. 2 pp.

317   _____: Part-time Employment. Bibliography P1C. New York:
      Catalyst, 1977. 4 pp.
         Together these three bibliographies list nearly 200
      books, articles, and government documents selected from the
      recent literature of business, the social sciences, and the
      women's movement. (For information on Catalyst, see 281.

318   BAYEFSKY, EVELYN. "Women and the Status of Part-time Work:
      A Review and Annotated Bibliography." Ontario Library
      Review 58 (June 1974):124-41; 61 (June 1977):87-106.
         The emphasis of the first literature review is on the
      rationale of part-time work. The author supplies long an-
      notations for 64 books and articles from Canada and the U.S.,
      most of them published after 1971, and lists another 18
      without annotation. The update deals more with policy
      questions and problems involved in implementing part-time
      work. It adds eighty-one citations for the period 1975-1977.

319   General Bibliography on Job Sharing. Palo Alto, Calif.: New
      Ways to Work, 1976. 13 pp. Addendum, 1977. 3 pp. Avail-
      able from New Ways to Work, 457 Kingsley Ave., Palo Alto,
      CA 94301.
         The combined bibliographies list over 200 books, period-
      ical and newspaper articles, unpublished papers, and state
      and federal documents. Writings cited come from scholarly,
      business, and feminist sources; most of them appeared after
      1960. There are occasional annotations.

320   NOLLEN, STANLEY D. New Patterns of Work. Studies in Produc-
      tivity: Highlights of the Literature, series 2, no. 7.
      Scarsdale, N.Y.: Work in America Institute, 1979. 59 pp.

Management

Bibliographies listed here are concerned with women managers in
a variety of occupations, most but not all related to business.
For bibliographies concerned solely with women administrators in
education, see Specific Occupations--Education.

321   PASK, JUDITH M. The Emerging Role of Women in Management:
       A Bibliography. West Lafayette, Ind.: Krannert Graduate
       School of Industrial Administration, Purdue University, 1976.
       49 pp. Available from EDRS, ED 132 490.
           This is a compilation of 523 references to women managers
       in the business world, largely selected from business liter-
       ature but also including general and social science publica-
       tions. The first part lists titles by format: Bibliog-
       aphies, Dissertations, Women's Periodicals and Special
       Issues, Audiovisual Materials, Historical and Statistical
       Background (a section including any titles published before
       1950). With minor exceptions materials cited in this part
       are not repeated in Part 2, a subject arrangement of books,
       articles, and government documents. The author index
       applies to both parts.

322   SWANICK, LYNNE STRUTHERS. Women as Administrators. Public
       Administration Series, no. P86. Monticello, Ill.: Vance
       Bibliographies, 1978. 16 pp.
           With the exception of a few outstanding items on women
       in educational administration, the 100-plus publications
       listed in this bibliography have to do with women in the
       business world of the U.S. and Canada. References include
       books, articles, dissertations, and government documents,
       most of them dated 1972 or later.

323   TERBORG, JAMES R. Integration of Women into Management
       Positions: A Research Review. Paper presented at the
       annual meeting of the American Psychological Association,
       Washington, September 3-7, 1976. Available from EDRS, ED
       132 708.
           The author reviews the literature on the psychological
       and social processes involved in the entry of women into
       management and their socialization after entry. The ac-
       companying list of about seventy entries concentrates on
       publications between 1973 and 1976, citing other literature
       reviews to cover earlier periods.

324   WILLIAMS, MARTHA; OLIVER, JEAN; and GERRARD, MEG. Women in
       Management: A Selected Bibliography. Austin: Center for
       Social Work Research, School of Social Work, University of
       Texas, 1977. 64 pp.
           The compilers state that "no pretense is made of total
       coverage of the literature" but offer instead a sampling
       that focuses on recent publications which can be obtained
       directly from the author or issuing agency. Some 650
       books, articles, and conference papers, more representative
       of social science than of business literature, are arranged
       in broad topical sections, each with a short introduction.

325 YARBOROUGH, JoANNE. Women in Management: Selected Recent
    References. Washington: U.S. Dept. of Labor Library, for
    sale by the Supt. of Docs., U.S. Govt. Print. Off., 1978.
    29 pp.
        This annotated selection of books, articles, and dis-
    sertations published from 1975 through 1977 also includes
    a few especially relevant older items. Because the data
    base The Information Bank was one source of citations, a
    number of newspaper articles not otherwise readily acces-
    sible are listed. In addition to general materials on
    women in management, the bibliography contains sections on
    women in business, in banking, on boards of directors, and
    in education.

Nontraditional Occupations

326 KOBA ASSOCIATES. Women in Non-traditional Occupations: A
    Bibliography. Washington: U.S. Office of Education,
    Bureau of Occupational and Adult Education, 1976. 189 pp.
    Available from EDRS, ED 133 460.
        Since, according to the 1970 census, women make up 38
    percent of the labor force, the compolers defined a non-
    traditional occupation as one in which women constitute
    less than 38 percent of the workers. Briefly annotated
    citations to magazine and journal articles, books, disserta-
    tions, pamphlets, brochures, and government documents are
    arranged in three main sections: general materials,
    skilled/vocational occupations (those not requiring a
    baccalaureate degree), and professional occupations (those
    calling for a degree). Appendixes list resources for ad-
    ditional information and sources for materials, and there
    are author, title, and subject indexes.

327 TACK, MARTHA WINGARD and ASHFORD, DEBORAH TAYLOR. Dimensions
    on Women's Employment in Non-Traditional Female Occupations:
    A Selected Bibliography, January 1970-July 1975. Washington:
    U.S. Office of Education, Bureau of Occupational and Adult
    Education, 1975. 85 pp. Available from EDRS, ED 123 490.
        Over 800 references on successful employment of women
    in nontraditional occupations (here defined as "all occupa-
    tions except those related to homemaking, nursing, elementary
    or secondary education, and stenography") are contained in
    this bibliography. It is based on a literature search
    designed to cover scholarly and popular periodicals,
    special women's publications, government documents, and
    dissertations as well as books and ERIC documents. Entries
    are listed by type of publication within four categories:
    articles, books, brochures/reports/government documents,
    and dissertations. There is no subject index, but each
    item is preceded by a number keyed to one of eighteen groups
    of occupations.

See also: 290.

Specific Occupations

Agriculture

328   FERA, DARLA. Women in American Agriculture: A Select Bib-
      liography. Library List 103. Beltsville, Md.: Economic
      Research Service and the National Agricultural Library,
      U.S. Dept. of Agriculture, 1977. 30 pp. Available from
      EDRS, ED 157 663.
         This briefly annotated alphabetical listing cites about
      170 books, articles, and government documents from the
      early twentieth century to 1977 dealing with "women engaged
      as landowners, farm managers, agricultural laborers, and in
      agricultural industries: beekeeping, silk culture, butter
      production, etc. References are included concerning women
      in agricultural education, as agricultural scientists, as
      workers in ag-related industries (not on the farm) and
      their involvement in rural organizations."

Architecture

329   DOUMATO, LAMIA. Women as Architects: A Historical View.
      Architecture Series, no. A6. Monticello, Ill.: Vance
      Bibliographies, 1978. 12 pp.
         Over 100 citations to books, articles from professional
      and feminist journals, exhibition catalogs, and newspaper
      articles are listed in three sections by period: nineteenth
      century, twentieth century to 1945, and 1945 to the present.
      A number of references are in foreign languages. Three
      final sections provide brief bibliographies on Louise
      Bethune, Marion Mahoney Griffin, and Julia Morgan.

330   HAYDEN, DOLORES and WRIGHT, GWENDOLYN. "Review Essay: Archi-
      tecture and Urban Planning." Signs 1 (Summer 1976):923-33.
         This article offers a selective consideration of recent
      research on women's participation in architecture and the
      physical aspects of urban planning and on the impact of
      environmental design on their lives and work, with sugges-
      tions for further research. The footnotes list about
      seventy-five studies, largely but not entirely dated 1970-
      1975.

331   JOHNSON, CAROLYN R. Women in Architecture: An Annotated
      Bibliography and Guide to Sources of Information. Exchange
      Bibliography 549. Monticello, Ill.: Council of Planning
      Librarians, 1974. 25 pp.
         In this bibliography about seventy-five books and
      articles from 1876 through 1973 are cited in four sections.
      Those on opportunities for women in the profession, their

achievements, and studies or surveys of women architects
are arranged chronologically, making their annotations
read like a brief history in themselves. The section on
careers in related fields is arranged by topic: art and
design, construction, planning, and landscape architecture.
Further chapters list organizations of women architects and
sources of statistics.

See also: 212.

Armed Forces

332   U.S. AIR FORCE ACADEMY. Library. Women in the Military.
       Comp. and ed. Betsy Coxe. Colorado Springs: U.S. Air
       Force Academy Library, 1975. 60 pp.
          The titles listed in this bibliography were selected
       from the Air Force Academy Library "to reflect the histori-
       cal development of women's roles and contributions in a
       traditionally male career field and to represent present
       day practices and problems." Writings on both U.S. and
       foreign servicewoman are organized in a subject arrangement
       subdivided by type of publication (books, periodical arti-
       cles, government documents, report literature). There are
       occasional brief annotations for titles needing clarifica-
       tion.

See also: 373.

Dentistry

333   BOQUIST, CONSTANCE and HAASE, JEANNETTE V. An Historical
       Review of Women in Dentistry: An Annotated Bibliography.
       Rockville, Md.: U.S. Public Health Service, Health Resources
       Administration, Office of Health Resources Opportunity,
       1977. 107 pp. Available from EDRS, ED 148 223.
          An alphabetical listing of 263 citations to articles in
       British, Canadian, and U.S. journals is followed by a
       chronological arrangement of abstracts for 162 of them
       ranging in date from 1865 to 1976. Most of the references
       are from the professional literature, but a few general
       publications are included.

Education

334   DONISI, PATRICIA. "Bibliography of Dissertations for and
       about Women in Administration in Colleges and Universities."
       In New Research on Women and Sex Roles at the University of
       Michigan. Ed. Dorothy G. McGuigan. Ann Arbor: Center for
       Continuing Education of Women, University of Michigan, 1976,
       pp. 322-31.
          A search of American Doctoral Dissertations and Disserta-
       tion Abstracts International for an unspecified period,
       seemingly 1950-1975, produced this list of eighty-two dis-
       sertations. It is arranged in ten topical sections with
       generous cross-references.

91

335   ESTLER, SUZANNE E.   "Women as Leaders in Public Education."
      Signs 1 (Winter 1975):363-86.
          The article proper is an examination of "the relative
      absence of women as leaders and the factors explaining this
      absence." It is followed by "Appendix A: Survey of the
      Literature" (pp. 378-80) and by a bibliography (pp. 380-86)
      citing over 150 published and unpublished writings, almost
      entirely dated since 1960.

336   HARMON, LINDA A.   Status of Women in Higher Education, 1963-
      1972: A Selective Bibliography.   Series in Bibliography,
      no. 2. Ames: Iowa State University Library, 1972.   124
      pp. Available from EDRS, ED 070 384.
          Women faculty and staff members, administrators, librar-
      ians, and students are the "women in higher education"
      referred to in the title. Publications about them are
      listed, with brief annotations, in chapters according to
      format: books, periodical articles, government documents,
      dissertations, ERIC resources, and ephemera. Although there
      is no index, the subject areas covered by each item are
      indicated by roman numerals corresponding to a set of
      subject headings.

337   KANE, ROSLYN D.   Sex Discrimination in Education: A Study of
      Employment Practices Affecting Professional Personnel.   Vol.
      2: Annotated Bibliography. Washington: U.S. National
      Center for Educational Statistics, 1976.   258 pp. Available
      from EDRS, ED 132 744.
          The emphasis of this bibliography is on original research,
      but some innovative secondary analyses and significant per-
      sonal commentaries are also included. Most of the writings
      listed were published between 1970 and 1975. The references
      are alphabetically arranged, each with a lengthy abstract
      outlining type of publication, population studied, date,
      method, findings, and recommendations. Two appendixes list
      studies of the status of women within specific academic
      disciplines and professions and at individual postsecondary
      institutions. There is a detailed subject index.

338   KILSON, MARION.   "Review Essay: The Status of Women in Higher
      Education." Signs 1 (Summer 1976):935-42.
          This analysis of the dominant trends for women's status
      in higher education cites about fifty titles, chiefly pub-
      lications of the mid-seventies, in footnotes.

339   Women in Educational Administration. Resource Roundup. San
      Francisco: Women's Educational Equity Communications Net-
      work, 1979.   6 pp. Available from Far West Laboratory for
      Educational Research and Development, 1855 Folsom St., San
      Francisco, CA 94103.

There are separate sections devoted to women administrators in higher and in elementary/secondary education in
this list of close to 100 papers, articles, reports, and
ERIC documents published in the 1970s. Only those items
whose titles are unclear have annotations, but notably full
information on availability is provided for all.

340 SILVER, DONNA and MAGEE, JANE. Women Administrators in Higher
     Education: A Selected Bibliography. Madison: School of
     Education, University of Wisconsin-Madison, 1978. 24 pp.
     Available from EDRS, ED 151 024.
        Although primarily concerned with the current status of
     women administrators in higher education, this bibliography
     also includes material on the history of women in academe,
     future trends for equal opportunity for women in this area,
     and the general issue of women and power. About 100 an-
     notated citations, almost all since 1970, are arranged in
     sections by format: books, journal articles, ERIC documents,
     and dissertations/proceedings/government documents.

See also: 261, 325.

Engineering

341 ROYSDON, CHRISTY. Women in Engineering: A Bibliography on
     Their Progress and Prospects. Exchange Bibliography 878.
     Monticello, Ill.: Council of Planning Librarians, 1975.
     22 pp.
        Because only three books treat the subject of women in
     engineering in depth, the compiler has included background
     materials discussing the professional woman in general.
     Other topical sections are concerned with status, recruit-
     ment, education and training, experience on the job, and
     role models. Materials listed include books, articles, and
     government documents. Aside from those titles calling for
     clarification, only outstanding items are annotated.

Geography

342 LOYD, BONNIE. Women and Geography: An Annotated Bibliography
     and Guide to Sources of Information. Exchange Bibliography
     1159. Monticello, Ill.: Council of Planning Librarians,
     1976. 18 pp.
        Two sections of roughly equal length make up this bib-
     liography: Women in the Discipline of Geography, and
     Geographic Studies of Women in Society. Both sections
     contain an assortment of print and nonprint titles, some
     briefly annotated.

Health Professions

See also Dentistry, Medicine, Nursing.

343   An Exploratory Study of Women in the Health Professions Schools.
Vol. 10, Annotated Bibliography. San Francisco: Urban and
Rural Systems Associates, 1976. 114 pp. Available from
NTIS, PB 259 234.

This bibliography lists materials reviewed in the preparation of a multi-volume study exploring the barriers
women face as applicants to and students in the schools of
the health professions. Generally found cited as above,
from its cover title, it is more accurately described on
its title page as "Bibliography and Annotated Bibliography,"
since over half its length consists of an unannotated
compilation of citations on both general topics, such as
women and careers, and specific health professions:
medicine, osteopathic medicine, dentistry, veterinary
medicine, optometry, podiatry, pharmacy, and public health.
The Annotated Bibliography that completes the volume is
made up of nearly 100 abstracts in one alphabetical sequence
touching on all the topics covered in the first section.
Materials cited come from a variety of academic, government,
and medical publications, with notable representation of
professional health organizations.

344   MAY, JEAN T. Health Career Databank for Minorities/Women:
Annotated Selected Bibliography. Pittsburgh: American
Institute for Research, 1976. 49 pp. Available from NTIS,
HRP 0019217.

"This bibliography represents an initial attempt at
selecting and compiling a part of the existing literature
from many different disciplines--public health, economics,
psychology, education, sociology. . .dealing with health
careers for minorities, women, and other disadvantaged
groups of our society." Citations to 357 books, articles,
government documents, and papers appearing between 1960 and
1975 are organized into seven topical sections, which are
annotated, and three sections by format (bibliographies,
Department of Labor and Census Bureau publications), which
are not annotated. A final section lists additional references received too late to annotate. Symbols in the margin
indicate the relevance of each title to women, minorities,
or both.

See also: 521, 524.

Journalism

345   MARZOLF, MARION; RUSH, RAMONA R.; and STERN, DARLENE. "The
Literature of Women in Journalism History." Journalism
History 1 (Winter 1974-75):117-28; Supp. Journalism History
3 (Winter 1976-77):116-20.

See also: 348.

Librarianship

346   "Bibliography" in <u>The Role of Women in Librarianship, 1876–</u>
      <u>1976: The Entry, Advancement, and Struggle for Equalization</u>
      <u>in One Profession</u>. Ed. Kathleen Weibel and Kathleen M.
      Heim. Phoenix: Oryx Press, 1979, pp. 295–503.
           The coverage of this annotated bibliography of over 400
      references to print and nonprint materials concentrates on
      women librarians in English-speaking countries, but its
      scope is international. (Foreign titles are given in both
      the original language and English translation.) It is based
      on a literature search so comprehensive that it supersedes
      most of the several earlier bibliographies on the subject.
      Thanks to its chronological arrangement and descriptive
      annotations it can be read, as its editors intended, "as a
      chronology of issues, themes, data, and opinions on the role
      of women in librarianship as well as a guide to literature."
      Access from other approaches is provided by subject, author,
      and title indexes.

347   CUMMINGS, CYNTHIA S. <u>A Biographical-Bibliographical Directory</u>
      <u>to Women Librarians</u>. Madison: Library School Women's
      Group, University of Wisconsin, 1976. [unpaginated] This
      bio-bibliography includes women librarians who have completed
      their careers or retired and are listed in the American
      Library Institute or in <u>Women in the Library Profession:</u>
      <u>Leadership Roles and Contributions</u>. The citations given
      consist of biographical materials plus any of the subject's
      own writings that deal with women. There are indexes by
      type of library and service. This work is not superseded
      by 346 because the latter excludes writings on individual
      women.

                                                    See also: 336.

      Mass Media

348   BEASLEY, MAURINE and SILVER, SHEILA. "Bibliographical Notes."
      In <u>Women in Media: A Documentary Source Book</u>. Washington:
      Women's Institute for Freedom of the Press, 1977, pp. 183–95.
           This series of brief bibliographic essays follows the
      organization of the book's text, covering works on women
      journalists in general, individual women printers and jour-
      nalists from the eighteenth to the twentieth centuries,
      black women journalists, early broadcasting, women's maga-
      zines, feminist periodicals, and a number of contemporary
      issues involving broadcasting, newspapers, advertising,
      and publishing. The sources given for each topic include
      manuscript collections and other primary materials as well
      as secondary treatments.

                                                    See also: 206.

Bibliographies

Medicine

349 MANDELBAUM, DOROTHY ROSENTHAL. "Review Essay: Women in Medicine." Signs 4 (Autumn 1978):136-45.
"The purpose of this review is to examine what has been written since 1973 about the individual woman physician and the situation of U.S. women in medicine." Topics considered include medicine as a nontraditional field for women, means of adaptation to the situation, identity conflict, and the motivation and personality of the individual woman physician. Citations to about sixty-five books, articles, and dissertations appear in the footnotes.

350 Women in Medicine: A Bibliography of the Literature on Women Physicians. Comp. and ed. Sandra L. Chaff et al. Metuchen, N.J.: Scarecrow Press, 1977. 1,124 pp.
Although the goal of this bibliography is comprehensive coverage of the literature on women physicians throughout the world, more than 90 percent of the 4,087 works cited are in English. (Titles for those in other languages are given in English translation only.) The references range in date from 1750 to 1975; their scope takes in women healers from earliest recorded history to the present time. Materials represented include books, articles from medical and nonmedical journals and from alumni/ae magazines, and dissertations. Since the bibliography is based on the Women in Medicine Collection of the Medical College of Pennsylvania, the compilers were able to examine over 95 percent of the entries for annotation. They are organized into fourteen subject sections subdivided geographically. Special sections worth noting are the biographies of nineteenth and twentieth century physicians and the selection of relevant works of fiction. There are also appendixes listing directories of women physicians and library collections on the subject, as well as author, subject, and personal name indexes.

*351 Bibliography of the History of Medicine. vol. 1- 1964-
Bethesda, Md.: National Library of Medicine, 1965- Annual with quinquennial cumulations.
This includes sections on women in medicine and on witchcraft.

See also: 522.

Nursing

352 FITZPATRICK, M. LOUISE. "Review Essay: Nursing." Signs 2 (Summer 1977):818-34.
Along with a historical overview of the profession and its major developments, the author discusses "selected publications of the last decade that focus on the problems of nursing as a women's profession, its relationships with

medicine, and the issues concerning the expanded role of the nurse." The footnotes cite about fifty books and articles.

353   Nurse Practitioners and the Expanded Role of the Nurse: A
      Bibliography. Nurse Planning Information Series, no. 5.
      Hyattsville, Md.:   Health Resources Administration, Division
      of Nursing, 1978.   253 pp.   Available from EDRS, ED 164
      511, also from NTIS, HRP 0500601.
         The National Health Planning Information Center, in
      response to frequent inquiries, created this bibliography
      by searching its own files, NTIS, Medline, and other auto-
      mated and manual sources. Abstracts as well as citations
      were retrieved where possible. All references include in-
      formation on availability; the majority are dated between
      1970 and 1977. They are grouped in broad categories:
      Expanded Role, Education, Acceptance, Evaluation, Health
      Care Delivery, and Manpower Planning. Although most of
      the literature represented comes from professional sources,
      it is not technical in nature.

   Police

354   DAVIS, LENWOOD G. The Policewoman in American Society: A
      Preliminary Survey. Exchange Bibliography 1045. Monticello,
      Ill.: Council of Planning Librarians, 1976. 14 pp.
         The principles of selection for this bibliography are not
      divulged, but it includes writings from the early twentieth
      century as well as those of more recent date. References
      are arranged in five sections by type of publication: books,
      articles, pamphlets, government documents, and theses/dis-
      sertations.

355   SHERMAN, MARION and SHERMAN, LEWIS J. "Bibliography on Police-
      women: 1945-1972." Law and Order 21 (March 1973):80-83.
         A large proportion of the 108 books, articles, and theses
      listed alphabetically in this bibliography come from profes-
      sional law enforcement literature.

                                                        See also: 373.
   Psychiatry

356   ROESKE, NANCY A. "Women in Psychiatry: A Review." American
      Journal of Psychiatry 133 (April 1976):365-72.
         This survey article considers women psychiatrists and
      the factors influencing their professional lives in both
      the U.S. and other developed countries, with special atten-
      tion to the situation of American women in psychiatry as
      of 1975. The seventy references come chiefly from medical
      and psychiatric literature.

Bibliographies

Science

357 ALDRICH, MICHELE L. "Review Essay: Women in Science." Signs
     4 (Autumn 1978):126-35.
          This survey of recent literature on women scientists is
     organized into sections on statistics, history of science,
     women as science students, and conferences and major studies.
     About forty publications, principally books and articles
     published since 1970, are cited in footnotes.

358 DAVIS, AUDREY B. Bibliography on Women: with Special Emphasis
     on Their Roles in Science and Society. New York: Science
     History Publications, 1974. 50 pp.
          This assortment of scholarly and popular books and a
     smaller number of periodical articles was compiled chiefly
     by selecting titles from the Library of Congress subject
     catalog. Although it contains about 600 titles, it is
     arranged alphabetically by author with no means of subject
     access.

359 KELLY, ALLISON. "Women in Science: A Bibliographical Review."
     Durham Research Review 7 (Spring 1976):1092-1108.
          The situation of women scientists in Britain and the
     world and the factors responsible for the small number of
     women scientists are the subject of this nonevaluative
     literature review. Educational factors are considered in
     greater detail than are social or psychological. The
     accompanying list of 131 references published since 1950
     concentrates on British publications but also includes some
     American and Australian studies.

360 U.S. LIBRARY OF CONGRESS. Science and Technology Division.
     Reference Section. Women in the Sciences. Comp. Constance
     Carter. LC Science Tracer Bullet, TB 76-2. Washington:
     Library of Congress, Science and Technology Division,
     Reference Section, 1976. 11 pp.
          Described as "a guide to sources chronicling the history
     and contributions of women in the field of science," this
     pamphlet not only gives highly selective lists of texts,
     reference books, geographical materials, government pub-
     lications, and conference proceedings, but also provides
     relevant subject headings in the card catalog, useful
     abstracting and indexing services with their headings, and
     guides to report literature.

                                              See also: 522.

Credit

361 RUPEN, ALICE; WAID, CANDACE; and BROWN, LESLIE. Women and
     Credit: An Annotated Bibliography. Washington: Center
     for Women Policy Studies, 1974. 27 pp.

References to recent publications in a variety of forms
make up this bibliography, and a separate section is devoted
to each form: newspaper and periodical articles, special
credit reports and surveys, government regulations, legal
documents, statements and testimony, published research,
unpublished papers. A final section cites writings on
labor force earnings and job turnover.

POLITICAL SCIENCE

Legal Status, Laws, etc.

Most of the bibliographies listed under Education and Employment
include materials on sex discrimination in those areas. Bibliographies on the legal aspects of abortion are included with other
bibliographies on abortion as a subsection of Health.

362   BROWN, RONALD L. "Common Law Marriage and the Legal Regulation
      of Cohabitation: A Bibliography." Women's Rights Law
      Reporter 4 (Spring 1978):187-95.

363   EQUAL RIGHTS AMENDMENT PROJECT. The Equal Rights Amendment:
      A Bibliographic Study. Westport, Conn.: Greenwood Press,
      1976. 367 pp.
         This work is a comprehensive listing of about 6,000
      publications dating from 1914 through January 1976. It is
      organized by format: congressional publications, other
      government documents, books and dissertations, pamphlets
      and brochures, periodical material (divided by type of
      periodical). The indexing of ten newspapers and the micro-
      film collections Herstory and Women and the Law, which lack
      topical indexes and complete reel guides, is worthy of note.
      Although there are no annotations, symbols indicate the
      nature and source of materials. There are both an author
      index and an organization index that includes addresses.

*364 Family Law Reporter. Washington: Bureau of National Affairs,
      1974- Weekly.
         This loose-leaf service is a fundamental current-awareness
      tool for legal questions related to marriage, divorce,
      domestic violence, and the family in general. It comes in
      four separate parts: Survey and Analysis (brief descrip-
      tions of state and federal court decisions), Courts and
      Legislatures (digests of opinions, legislation, and reports),
      Text (full text of U.S. Supreme Court opinions and other
      especially significant items), Monographs (articles on
      subjects of timely interest). In addition to the detailed
      cumulative index, each issue contains a table of cases,
      state table, and topical summary.

365   HUGHES, MARIJA MATICH. "Women's Rights: A Selected Bibliog-
      raphy." International Journal of Law Libraries 4 (Nov.
      1976):216-48.
          Compiled to facilitate research and publication in inter-
      national legal literature, this bibliography includes mater-
      ials published from 1970 through 1975 in the original
      language of publication with the exception of Chinese and
      Japanese. (Since Hughes's The Sexual Barrier (002) lists
      English-language writings only, the larger work does not
      supersede this one.) Three appendixes follow the bibliog-
      raphy: List of International Women's Organizations Con-
      sulted; Notes on Organizations Which Publish in the Field
      of Women's Rights (with annotated lists of their publica-
      tions); UNESCO Reports, Studies, and Publications on Women.

366   "Preliminary Selected Checklist On Legal Aspects Of Sex and
      Sex Based Discrimination." Record of the Association of
      the Bar of the City of New York 26 (Nov. 1971):711-42.
          This compilation of about 600 citations is made up
      chiefly of articles from legal periodicals, but it also
      lists a number of social science publications and govern-
      ment documents. Each of its three main sections (general,
      family law, and sex based discrimination) is broken down
      into topical subsections, including one giving thirty-one
      references on women in the legal profession.

*367 Reporter on Human Reproduction and the Law. Boston: Legal-
      Medical Studies, Inc., 1972/73-
          The subtitle of this loose-leaf service describes it as
      "a regular, accurate up-dating of materials on the legal,
      medical, ethical, and social developments in: abortion,
      artificial insemination, conception control, medical mal-
      practice, the family and reproduction." The issues examined
      consist of references to legal materials, chiefly judicial
      decisions, on abortion, birth control, pregnancy, and child-
      birth.

368   ROUNDTREE, DOVEY. "Equal Opportunity for Women in Housing:
      A Bibliography." In Women and Housing: A Report on Sex
      Discrimination in Five American Cities. Washington: Office
      of Assistant Secretary for Fair Housing and Equal Opportu-
      nity, Housing and Urban Development Dept.; for sale by
      Supt. of Docs., U.S. Govt. Print. Off., 1976, pp. 175-96.
          This partially annotated bibliography, topically arranged,
      cites 168 publications on women's legal, social, and eco-
      nomic position in seeking housing. The materials listed
      include statutes, judicial decisions, regulations, hearings,
      and commentaries from a variety of legal and general sources,
      with some emphasis on the states of California, Georgia,
      Missouri, New York, and Texas.

*369   Sexual Law Reporter. Los Angeles. vol. 1- 1975- Quarterly.
       A loose-leaf service published with the assistance of
       the National Committee for Sexual Civil Liberties, this
       serial is particularly useful for maintaining current
       awareness of legal matters concerned with unconventional
       sex. Each issue is made up of reports on state and federal
       court opinions, public and private administrative rulings,
       and legislation. There are occasional longer review arti-
       cles, reprints of documents, and bibliographies as well as
       an annual subject index and table of cases.

370   Women's Rights Law Reporter. vol. 1- Newark, N.J.: Rutgers
       University Law School, 1971- Quarterly.
       A bibliography of recent law review articles on women's
       rights appeared regularly from 1972 through 1976, covering
       articles published from 1971 through summer 1976. At this
       point it was dropped from the periodical, although a
       twenty-page list of articles published from September 1976
       through September 1977 was announced as available. See
       Women's Rights Law Reporter 4 (Winter 1978):58.

See also: 020, 110.

Politics

371   ENGELBARTS, RUDOLF. Women in the United States Congress,
       1917-1972: Their Accomplishments; with Bibliographies.
       Littleton, Colo.: Libraries Unlimited, 1975. 184 pp.
       Biographical sketches of the eighty-one women who served
       in Congress between 1917 and 1972, each with a bibliography
       of books and articles by and about the woman, constitute
       the main part of this book. They are supplemented by a
       thirty-one-page partially annotated bibliography on American
       women in general and women in politics in England, Germany,
       and the U.S. This is topically arranged with an author
       index for books cited but none for articles. A concluding
       name and subject index applies to the biobibliography only.

372   KRAUSS, WILMA RULE. "Political Implications of Gender Roles:
       A Review of the Literature." American Political Science
       Review 68 (December 1974):1706-23.
       This review essay covers published books and articles
       of the previous five years and some reprints of classic
       statements on the subject. The bibliography cites over
       200 titles in three parts: literature explicating gender
       roles, life cycles, and economic and social factors related
       to political participation, historical background, and
       origins of gender relationships.

373   LEVENSON, ROSALINE. <u>Women in Government and Politics: A</u>
<u>Bibliography of American and Foreign Sources</u>. Exchange
Bibliography 491. Monticello, Ill.: Council of Planning
Librarians, 1973. 80 pp.
      Except for some earlier titles of special importance,
this bibliography of books and articles is limited to works
published since 1940. It is organized into four sections:
Bibliographies and Indexes; Women in Government (including
the armed forces, federal employment, the police, and state
and local government); Women in Politics; Women in Government
and Politics in Other Countries.

374   STANWICK, KATHY and LI, CHRISTINE. <u>The Political Participation</u>
<u>of Women in the United States: A Selected Bibliography,</u>
<u>1950-1976</u>. Metuchen, N.J.: Scarecrow Press, 1977. 169 pp.
      Prepared at the Center for the American Woman and
Politics of Rutgers University, this bibliography is "the
result of a systematic attempt to assembly citations to all
materials available on American women's political participation at both mass and elite levels." Items focusing on
specific issues such as abortion are included only if they
also consider women's political activity on these issues.
Both published and unpublished writings produced between
1950 and 1976 as well as work in progress are listed, but
newspaper articles and most articles from popular magazines
are excluded. The 1,548 references are grouped by format
with author and biographical indexes but no further access
by topic.

375   WHALEY, SARA S. "American Women in National Politics."
<u>Women Studies Abstracts</u> 1 (Spring 1972):1-9, 88-97.
      This bibliographic essay cites about sixty books and
articles on the role of women in the national government,
political parties, and pressure groups. Emphasis is on
the current situation and most of the entries are dated
since 1960.

See also: 78, 79, 287, 482.

<u>Violence Against Women</u>

This section includes bibliographies concerned with general
violence against women or with woman battering. Bibliographies
dealing solely with rape are listed in the section that follows.

376   ABRAMSON, CATHERINE. <u>Spouse Abuse: An Annotated Bibliography</u>.
Washington: Center for Women Policy Studies, 1977. [20]
pp.
      The viewpoints of behavioral scientists, feminists,
police, lawyers, and crisis intervention personnel are all
represented in the fifty-odd annotated citations and the

unannotated list of about 150 suggested additional readings. A few films and television programs are included along with published and unpublished materials; most, but not all, date from the 1970s.

377   HOWARD, PAMELA F. Wife Beating: A Selected, Annotated Bibliography. San Diego, Calif.: Current Bibliography Series, 1978. 57 pp. Available from Current Bibliography Series, P.O. Box 2709, San Diego, CA 92112.
       This annotated bibliography lists 140 printed items in categories by format (books/pamphlets, periodical articles, newspaper articles, newsbank, government publications) with additional sections listing 5 films and 17 agencies from which printed material is available on request.

378   LYSTAD, MARY HANEMANN. "Violence at Home: A Review of the Literature." American Journal of Orthopsychiatry 45 (April 1975):328-45.
       This survey reviews studies of family violence in general and of spouse abuse, child abuse, and abuse by children. The 162 references, largely materials published since 1960, come from the literature of medicine, law, and criminology as well as from the social and behavioral sciences and include a number of foreign sources.

379   _____. Violence at Home: An Annotated Bibliography. Rockville, Md.: National Institute of Mental Health; for sale by Supt. of Docs., U.S. Govt. Print. Off., 1974. 95 pp.
       Nearly 200 scientific studies of family violence are abstracted in this bibliography. They include books, articles, dissertations, and conference papers, chiefly published within the previous ten years. The topical chapters into which they are grouped deal with the different family members involved as well as the incidence of family violence, its relation to other social issues, and the need and effectiveness of social services to meet the problem. There are ample cross-references and an author index.

380   McSHANE, CLAUDETTE. Annotated Bibliography on Woman Battering. Milwaukee: Center for Advanced Studies in Human Services, School of Social Welfare, University of Wisconsin, 1977. 25 pp.
       Directed toward both professionals and nonprofessionals, this bibliography contains citations to academic research, clinical reports, feminist writings, popular periodical articles, and practical handbooks. Newspaper articles are omitted. About 125 references are organized by type of material, with annotated titles preceding a smaller number without annotations in each section.

381   PETHICK, JANE. "A Bibliography on Battered Wives." In
      Domestic Violence: Issues and Dynamics. Ed. Vincent
      D'Oyley. Toronto: Ontario Institute for Studies in Educa-
      tion, 1978, pp. 229-48.
          This selected bibliography lists about 165 items, mainly
      American, British, or Canadian writings published since
      1970. The Canadian references are mostly newspaper articles
      and are starred. Titles are arranged by format: books,
      scholarly articles, reports/theses/pamphlets, periodicals/
      special issues, newspaper and magazine articles.

382   STAHLY, GERALDINE BUTTS. "A Review of Select Literature of
      Spousal Violence." Victimology 2, nos. 3-4 (1977):591-607.
          The emphasis of this literature review is on "empirical
      data concerning the frequency, demography, and interper-
      sonal process variables related to spousal violence." The
      forty references listed include studies made from 1930
      through 1976.

383   WILSON, CAROLYN F. and CLARENBACH, KATHRYN F. Violence against
      Women: Causes and Prevention: A Literature Search and
      Annotated Bibliography. Madison: Women's Education
      Resources, University of Wisonsin-Extension, 1979. 36 pp.
          From more than 800 articles, studies, and surveys yielded
      by a computer search of the Psychological Abstracts, Medlars,
      and National Institute of Mental Health data bases for the
      years 1970-1977, about ninety were selected for this bibliog-
      raphy. Most of them represent professional journal litera-
      ture. Emphasis is on general violence against women, rape,
      and woman battering; and separate treatments of incest,
      prostitution, and sexual harassment at work are excluded.
      Most of the work is organized by discipline, with separate
      listings of cross-cultural, criminological, medical, psycho-
      logical, and sociological studies. This makes it difficult
      to locate titles referred to in the literature review that
      precedes the bibliography, since there is no author index.

Rape

384   ALBIN, ROCHELLE SEMMEL. "Review Essay: Psychological Studies
      of Rape." Signs 3 (Winter 1977):423-35.
          "In few other contexts have women been as maligned, as
      degraded, and yet as ignored as in discussions of rape by
      mental health professionals. Description of the histori-
      cal antecedents of this situation can lead to development
      of the theoretical framework that analyses of rape currently
      lack." The writings covered in this survey extend from
      Freud to the new feminist research. Nearly 100 citations
      to the professional literature of psychology and criminology,
      including a number of unpublished papers, appear in the
      footnotes.

385 BARNES, DOROTHY L. <u>Rape: A Bibliography</u>, 1965-1975. Troy, N.Y.: Whitston Publishing Co., 1977. 154 pp.
    The preface describes this as a "virtually comprehensive list of books and journal articles" for the period, and from the list of sources consulted, this would appear to be true. References are arranged in four sections. The first lists about 100 books (including some government documents and foreign sources) alphabetically by author. The second section cites nearly 700 journal articles in alphabetical order by title. The third section rearranges the same articles under 126 subject headings, and the fourth is an author index to the articles only.

386 CHAPPELL, DUNCAN; GEIS, GILBERT; and FOGARTY, FAITH. "Forcible Rape: Bibliography." <u>Journal of Criminal Law and Criminology</u> 65 (June 1974):248-63.
    The compilers introduce this bibliography with comment on the change in emphasis of the literature on rape caused by the women's movement and the importance of bibliographic control as a step towards integration and reexamination of the subject. References to 333 medical, legal, feminist, and behavioral science publications are grouped in a classified arrangement with cross-references and an author index. For a continuation, <u>see</u> 389.

387 EVANS, HANNAH I. and SPEREKAS, NICOLE B. "Sexual Assault Bibliography, 1920-1975." <u>Catalog of Selected Documents in Psychology</u> 6 (November 1976):112. MS 1368. 60 pp.
    This extensive bibliography cites about 1,500 books, articles, and conference papers in alphabetical order without access by subject. Emphasis is on adult rape, but child victimization and incest are also considered. The references come from medical, legal, and psychological literature as well as from the popular press and include a notable number of foreign publications. (Foreign titles are translated into English.)

    Continued by:

388 EVANS, HANNAH I. "Sexual Assault Bibliography: Update and Expansion." <u>Catalog of Selected Documents in Psychology</u> 7 (August 1977):78. MS 1535. 13 pp.
    This continuation adds 227 references--covering the years 1976 and 1977--to the earlier bibliography by Evans and Sperekas.

389 FEILD, HUBERT S. and BARNETT, NONA J. "Forcible Rape: An Updated Bibliography." <u>Journal of Criminal Law and Criminology</u> 68 (March 1977):146-59.

This is an update of the bibliography by Chappell, Geis,
and Fogarty (386), using the same classified format and
including sources published from 1974 through 1976.

390   KEMMER, ELIZABETH JANE. Rape and Rape-Related Issues: An
      Annotated Bibliography. New York: Garland Publishing,
      1977. 174 pp.
         Covering English-language literature on rape published
      from 1965 through summer of 1976, this bibliography lists
      348 books, chapters from books, and periodical articles
      alphabetically by author with a subject index. A list of
      periodicals represented is included; they range from medi-
      cal and legal literature to the popular women's magazines.
      A detailed annotation, almost an abstract, is provided for
      each entry.

391   The Rape Bibliography: A Collection of Abstracts. St. Louis:
      St. Louis Feminist Research Project, 1976. 93 pp. Available
      from St. Louis Feminist Research Project, 4431 McPherson,
      St. Louis, MO 63108.
         Not all the entries in this work have abstracts. Its
      more than 500 references are organized in five major
      sections: Legal, Medical, Psychological, Sociological, and
      Popular Press. Each of these is subdivided into Bibliography
      (citations for materials written before 1970) and Abstracts
      (summaries of scholarly books and articles in English pub-
      lished after 1970, plus a few especially important earlier
      works.) A brief list of pamphlets concludes the bibliog-
      raphy.

392   WALKER, MARCIA J. Toward the Prevention of Rape: A Partially
      Annotated Bibliography. University: Center for Correctional
      Psychology, University of Alabama, 1975. 104 pp. Available
      from National Criminal Justice Microfiche Program,
      NCJ-16783.

ANTHROPOLOGY

General

*393 International Bibliography of Social and Cultural Anthropology.
      vol. 1- London: Tavistock Publications; Chicago: Aldine
      Publishing Co., 1955- Annual.
         Three sections of this continuing bibliography apply
      especially to women: Marriage, Sexual Relations and Be-
      haviour, Traditional Status Relations between the Sexes.

394 LAMPHERE, LOUISE. "Review Essay: Anthropology." <u>Signs</u> 2
      (Spring 1977):612-27.
          This literature review for the period 1974-1976 con-
      centrates on "theoretical issues within socio-cultural
      anthropology and the study of sex roles." The footnotes
      list about forty books, articles, and unpublished papers.

395 QUINN, NAOMI. "Anthropological Studies on Women's Status."
      <u>Annual Review of Anthropology</u> 6 (1977):181-225.
          The various explanations offered for the similarities
      and differences in women's status between societies are
      described and the hypotheses represented are evaluated in
      this literature review. The accompanying list of ninety-one
      references comprises largely scholarly publications issued
      since 1970.

396 RAPP, RAYNA. "Review Essay: Anthropology." <u>Signs</u> 4 (Spring
      1979):497-513.
          About 125 scholarly publications appearing between 1976
      and 1978 are covered in this review essay. A number of them
      are themselves literature reviews, bibliographies, or area
      overviews.

397 REITER, RAYNA. "Anthropological Perspectives on Women:
      Selected Bibliography." In <u>Female Studies</u> 7: <u>Going Strong</u>:
      <u>New Courses/New Programs</u>. Ed. Deborah Silverton Rosenfelt.
      Old Westbury, N.Y.: Feminist Press, 1973, pp. 121-7.
          This reading list for a graduate seminar in anthropology
      cites nearly 300 books and articles in a classified arrange-
      ment that has both topical and geographical sections. Al-
      though shorter than Jacobs's <u>Women in Perspective</u> (003),
      it lists a number of titles not included there.

398 STACK, CAROL B. et al. "Review Essay: Anthropology." <u>Signs</u>
      1 (Autumn 1975):147-59.
          This review of anthropological research on women is
      concerned chiefly with work done between 1970 and mid-1975
      in the major areas of human evolution, symbolism, linguis-
      tics, and social organization. References appear only in
      the seventy-seven footnotes.

See also: 003.

Witchcraft

399 KEENEY, STEVEN H. "Witchcraft in Colonial Connecticut and
      Massachusetts: An Annotated Bibliography." <u>Bulletin of</u>
      <u>Bibliography</u> 33 (Feb.-Mar. 1976):61-72.
          This bibliography supplies evaluative annotations for
      about 200 scholarly books and articles concerned directly
      with the topic and published between the seventeenth

century and the 1970s. The first section consists of five
bibliographies; the second lists all the other titles in
one alphabetical sequence.

400 NUGENT, DONALD. "Witchcraft Studies, 1959-1971: A Bibliog-
     raphic Survey." Journal of Popular Culture 5 (Winter
     1971):710-25. Reprinted in The Occult: Studies and Eval-
     uations. Ed. Robert Galbreath. Bowling Green, Ohio:
     Bowling Green Popular Press, 1972.
        The focus of this bibliography is on historical studies,
     with some mention of works in related fields such as anthro-
     pology, religion, and abnormal psychology. Other bibliog-
     raphies and their relation to this one are specified.
     Organization is by historical periods, including contempo-
     rary times. The works cited are in French and German as
     well as in English, and most of them are books.

For a continuing bibliography that carries a section on witchcraft
see *351.

SOCIOLOGY

General

401 FRANSELLA, FAY and FROST, KAY. On Being a Woman: A Review of
     Research on How Women See Themselves. London: Tavistock
     Publications, 1977. 237 pp.
        This work is a book-length literature review keyed to
     a list of over 300 references, principally British and
     American sociological and psychological books and articles
     published since 1960. The eleven chapters are built around
     such topics as social definition of a woman's place, women's
     thinking on woman's place and on women's personalities,
     the development of sex role perceptions, women's self-esteem,
     sex, pregnancy and childbirth, mental health, and sex stereo-
     types. The chief value of the book, considering the rather
     small number of publications it covers, lies in the authors'
     extensive analyses and their comparisons of works on related
     topics. There are name and subject indexes.

402 HUBER, JOAN. "Review Essay: Sociology." Signs 1 (Spring
     1976):685-97.
        "This review of sociological research on women published
     from September 1973 to September 1975. . .covers the work
     only of trained sociologists, only fifty-eight English-
     language journals, and only those new books listed in the
     book review journal of the American Sociological Associa-
     tion, the Canadian Newsletter of Research on Women, or in
     recent bibliographies on women in economic development and
     on sex roles." The footnotes cite about 140 items.

*403   International Bibliography of Sociology/Bibliographie inter-
         nationale de sociologie. vol. 1- London: Tavistock
         Publications; Chicago: Aldine Publishing Co., 1951-
         Annual.
              A number of sections in this continuing bibliography
         apply particularly to women, notably: Household/Man/Woman,
         Family Planning, Marriage/Family, Sexual Behaviour, Family,
         Women's Status, Woman Worker/Young Worker.

404   LOPATA, HELENA ZNANIECKI. "Review Essay: Sociology." Signs
        2 (Autumn 1976):165-76.
              Emphasis of this selective review is on the sociological
        literature of 1975, including as topics the family, the
        life course, occupations and social stratification, and
        sexual identity research. The footnotes cite about eighty
        books and articles.

405   SERUYA, FLORA C.; LOSHER, SUSAN; and ELLIS, ALBERT. Sex and
        Sex Education: A Bibliography. New York: R. R. Bowker,
        1972. 336 pp.
              This international English-language bibliography of over
        2,000 titles attempts to bring together the most significant
        work on sexology, including both recent research and older
        work valuable for its historical perspective. The approach
        is primarily psychological/sociological, with medical
        literature represented chiefly by historical items and the
        section on literature made up mostly of literary criticism
        rather than belles-lettres. Citations for books, pamphlets,
        and special issues of newspapers (note the absence of
        journal articles) are listed in a detailed topical arrange-
        ment. There are occasional annotations to clarify ambiguous
        titles, and author, title, and subject indexes.

See also: 418, 493.

Sex Roles

406   ASTIN, HELEN S.; PARELMAN, ALICE; and FISHER, ANNE. Sex Roles:
        A Research Bibliography. Rockville, Md.: National Insti-
        tute of Mental Health, 1975. 362 pp. Available from EDRS,
        ED 112 306.
              Intended to provide an overview rather than a critical
        review of the research literature on sex roles, this bib-
        liography selects 456 titles ranging in date from 1960 to
        1972 to represent the different theories and methodologies
        concerned. Three-fourths of the entries are journal arti-
        cles, chiefly from the social and behavioral sciences. The
        references are grouped into five categories: Sex Differ-
        ences, The Development of Sex Differences, Specialized Sex
        Roles in Institutional Settings, Cross-cultural Overviews,
        Reviews and Theoretical Expositions. Each item has both
        a lengthy abstract and a set of subject descriptors, and
        there are author and subject indexes.

407 HOCHSCHIELD, ARLIE RUSSELL. "A Review of Sex Role Research."
    American Journal of Sociology 78 (Jan. 1973):1011-29.
    Reprinted in Changing Women in a Changing Society. Ed.
    Joan Huber. Chicago: University of Chicago Press, 1973,
    pp. 57-76.
        "This review is offered as a guide to the questions and
    theoretical starting points of four types of research on
    sex roles": research on sex differences (much of it done
    by psychologists but cited by sociologists), sex roles,
    women as a minority group, and the politics of caste. Most
    of the 105 books and articles listed are academic sociolog-
    ical works published after 1960, and twenty-four of them
    are other literature reviews or annotated bibliographies.

408 KATZ, LILIAN G. et al. Sex Role Socialization in Early Child-
    hood. Urbana: ERIC Clearinghouse on Early Childhood Edu-
    cation, University of Illinois, 1977. 107 pp. Available
    from EDRS, ED 148 472.

409 _____. Sex Role Socialization in Early Childhood: An Anno-
    tated Bibliography. Urbana: ERIC Clearinghouse on Early
    Childhood Education, 1977. 76 pp. Available from EDRS,
    ED 148 473.
        The first of these, a literature review focusing on the
    influence of the family, the mass media, and the school,
    comments on 167 items. All of these titles are included
    in the second, a more comprehensive and completely anno-
    tated bibliography. Its 321 entries, chiefly published
    between 1970 and 1977, are organized into five categories:
    General Interest, Media, School, Family, Curriculum
    Materials.

410 LIPMAN-BLUMEN, JEAN and TICKAMYER, ANN R. "Sex Roles in
    Transition: A Ten-Year Perspective." Annual Review of
    Sociology 1 (1975):297-337.
        This literature review covers scholarly work published
    for the most part between 1964 and 1974, although the list
    of over 350 references contains titles from the 1950s and
    even earlier. The large number of section and subsection
    headings in the text makes it easy to locate titles on any
    particular topic.

See also: 205, 258, 372, 436.

Marriage and Family

411 ALDOUS, JOAN and HILL, REUBEN. International Bibliography of
    Research in Marriage and the Family. Minneapolis: Uni-
    versity of Minnesota Press for the Minnesota Family Study
    Center and the Institute of Life Insurance. vol. 1,
    1900-1964, 1967. vol. 2, 1965-1972, comp. Joan Aldous
    and Nancy Dahl, 1974.

This massive computer-produced bibliography of over 25,000 titles attempts a comprehensive listing of "every research item published since 1900 in which some manifestation of marriage or the family figured," including monographs, pamphlets, bulletins, parts of books, and journal articles. Non-English citations make up 12 percent of the first volume, 40 percent of the second. The organization of the two volumes differs slightly, but each provides author, subject, and keyword indexing. For a continuation, see *415.

412   BAGLEY, CHRISTOPHER. "Inter-Ethnic Marriage in Britain and the United States from 1970-1977: A Selected Abstract Bibliography." Sage Race Relations Abstracts 4 (Feb. 1979): 1-22.
        Most of the fifty-five references in this bibliography have to do with interracial marriage. They include books and articles selected principally from social science literature and listed in a detailed topical arrangement.

413   CAVAN, RUTH SHONLE. "Annotated Bibliography of Studies on Intermarriage in the United States, 1960-1970 Inclusive." International Journal of Sociology of the Family 1 (Special Issue, May 1971):157-65.

414   GURMAN, ALAN S. "Marital Therapy: A Content-Coded Bibliography, 1928-1972." Catalog of Selected Documents in Psychology 3 (Spring 1973):55. MS 366. 47 pp.
        In this bibliography, citations to 451 books, articles, and unpublished papers on the clinical-theoretical and research aspects of marital therapy are coded according to one or more of eighteen specific content categories but are not otherwise annotated.

*415   Inventory of Marriage and Family Literature. vol. 3- 1973/74- St. Paul: Family Social Science, University of Minnesota, 1975- Annual.
        Continuing International Bibliography of Research in Marriage and the Family (411) and assuming its volume numbering, this serial bibliography covers English-language materials only but lists all relevant articles published in professional journals and is not restricted to research and theory as were the first two volumes.

416   LAWS, JUDITH LONG. "A Feminist Review of the Marital Adjustment Literature: The Rape of the Locke." Journal of Marriage and the Family 33 (August 1971):483-516.
        This bibliographic essay analyzes published research in terms of its findings, its methodology, and the areas it neglects. Almost all the 168 references are dated between 1950 and 1971.

*417   Marriage and Family Review. vol. 1- 1978- New York: Haworth
       Press, 1978- Bimonthly.
            The bulk of each issue is made up of about 100 abstracts
       from the technical journal literature. They cover the core
       journals in the field of marriage and the family intensively
       and also list pertinent articles from peripheral journals
       indexed in Social Science Citation Index and Science Citation
       Index. Abstracts are arranged by journal with a subject
       index which cumulates the entries for the issues in each
       volume until the volume is complete.

 418   MINNESOTA COUNCIL ON FAMILY RELATIONS. Family Life: Litera-
       ture and Films, an Annotated Bibliography. Minneapolis:
       the Council, 1972. 353 pp.
            This multi-media bibliography, which has appeared in
       successive editions since 1951, cites materials for use by
       family members and professionals concerned with family
       problems as well as works useful for research. Its scope
       is wider than the title indicates: the main divisions deal
       with the family; sexuality, sex roles, and sex education;
       human reproduction and family planning; adolescence; court-
       ship and mate selection; marital and family interaction;
       family crises (including divorce and death); child develop-
       ment and parenthood; middle and later years; self-growth
       and human potential; social issues (including drug abuse
       and delinquency); and family life education. Each of these
       is subdivided topically and further divided by form of
       material. An appendix contains lists of periodicals, pub-
       lishers, and audiovisual sources as well as an author index.

*419   Sage Family Studies Abstracts. vol.1- Beverly Hills, Calif.:
       1979- Quarterly.
            Each issue abstracts about 250 books, articles, pamphlets,
       government documents, and other publications, with special
       effort made to include dissertations, speeches, and similar
       fugitive materials. Entries are organized in a subject
       arrangement whose main sections are: Theory and Methodology;
       Lifestyles; Life Cycles; Marital and Family Processes;
       Problems, Therapy, and Counseling; Sex Roles; Social Issues.
       Each of these sections is subdivided topically. In addi-
       tion, there is an alphabetical list of about seventy-five
       unannotated citations. The author and subject indexes
       cover only the abstracts.

 420   SCHLESINGER, BENJAMIN. The One-Parent Family: Perspectives
       and Annotated Bibliography. 3d ed. Toronto: University
       of Toronto Press, 1975. 186 pp.
            The first third of this book is made up of essays by
       Schlesinger on the one-parent family in Canada, Australia,
       and Great Britain and an essay by Jetse Sprey on the

methodology of studying single parenthood. Each of these
has a brief reference list. The annotated bibliography
which constitutes the central third of the work repeats
535 citations for 1930–1969 from an earlier edition and
adds a section covering the years 1970–1974. Both sections
use the same topical arrangement. The book concludes with
a series of statistical appendixes on one-parent families
in Canada, the U.S., and Great Britain, a brief essay, with
references, analyzing family research on remarriage in
America, a list of publishers, and an author index.

421   SCHUSTER, ELIZABETH and SCOTT, MELVIA. <u>Executives' Wives and</u>
       <u>Mobile Families</u>. Toledo, Ohio: Business Research Center,
       College of Business Administration, University of Toledo,
       1976. 3 pp.
           This little bibliography includes over thirty citations
       to books, articles, and unpublished papers, most of them
       from business literature.

See also: 71, 89, 116, 246, 269,
362, 364, 426, 430, 432, 548.

History of the Family

422   BERKNER, LUTZ K. "Recent Research on the History of the
       Family in Western Europe." <u>Journal of Marriage and the</u>
       <u>Family</u> 35 (Aug. 1973):395–405.
           This review essay examines research in three areas:
       social classes, demography, and local/regional studies.
       The reference list cites about 130 scholarly writings,
       mostly English-language publications since 1960 but also
       including some in foreign languages and others as early
       as the mid-nineteenth century.

423   CREMIN, LAWRENCE A. "The Family as Educator: Some Comments
       on the Recent Historiography." <u>Teachers College Record</u>
       76 (Dec. 1974):250–65.
           The history of the American family is the focus of this
       literature review. Works listed in its bibliography of
       nearly 100 items are, except for those in the first sec-
       tion, dated since 1960. The arrangement is by format:
       Five Classic Studies, Bibliographical and Methodological
       Analyses, Anthologies and Periodicals, Published Monographs,
       Unpublished Monographs.

424   MILDEN, JAMES WALLACE. <u>The Family in Past Time: A Guide to</u>
       <u>the Literature</u>. New York: Garland Publishing, 1977.
       200 pp.
           This is the most extensive bibliography on family
       history. Although lists only writings in English, its
       scope is worldwide. More than 1,300 books, articles,

unpublished papers, and theses appearing between the late
nineteenth century and the close of 1975 are listed in an
elaborate subject arrangement: geographical chapters are
divided by period and further divided by topic. (One of
the topics in each of these subdivisions is Women.) The
introduction gives an overview of the significance and
development of family history and areas of needed research,
and individual titles have descriptive annotations. There
is an author index.

425   SINOFSKY, FAYE; FITZPATRICK, JOHN J.; POTTS, LOUIS W.; and
       de MAUSE, LLOYD. "A Bibliography of Psychohistory. Sec-
       tion 2: The History of Childhood." History of Childhood
       Quarterly 2 (Spring 1975):530-41.
           The chief value of this alphabetical listing of over
       300 books, articles, dissertations, and unpublished papers
       now lies in its inclusion of a number of non-English titles.

Ethnic and Racial Groups

Black Women

426   DAVIS, LENWOOD G. The Black Family in the United States: A
       Selected Bibliography of Annotated Books, Articles, and
       Dissertations on Black Families in America. Westport,
       Conn.: Greenwood Press, 1978. 132 pp.
           The nearly 400 citations of this bibliography are organ-
       ized in four sections: an alphabetical listing of 62 Major
       Books, and topically arranged sections of General Books
       (about 150 titles), Articles (about the same number), and
       Dissertations (about 75 titles). General and social science
       literature as well as a number of periodicals identifying
       themselves as black are included; most publications are
       dated since 1950. All annotations for books and articles
       conclude with a brief evaluation, but annotations for dis-
       sertations are descriptive only. There are author and
       subject indexes.

427   _____. The Black Woman in American Society: A Selected,
       Annotated Bibliography. Boston: G.K. Hall, 1975. 159 pp.
           In this bibliography of over 700 entries, only the
       sections devoted to books and articles are annotated.
       Other sections listing reference works, periodicals, and
       reports or documents give citations only. Both contemporary
       and historical materials are included, and the coverage of
       individual biographies is especially strong. In addition
       to the bibliographical references, there are lists of
       libraries, organizations, publishers/editors, and elected
       officials, as well as statistics and an author/subject
       index.

428   DUNMORE, CHARLOTTE J. Black Children and Their Families: A
       Bibliography. San Francisco: R and E Research Associates,
       1976. 103 pp.
           Although the focus of this bibliography is on black
       children rather than on their families, several of its
       nine topical chapters relate to families and women, notably
       Family Life (about 300 references) and Sex, Contraception,
       and Family Planning (about 60 references). Except for
       classic titles from an earlier period, the works cited are
       academic and professional literature published since 1960.
       Some racist materials have been included deliberately in
       order to present as wide a range as possible.

429   JACKSON, JACQUELYNE JOHNSON. "A Partial Bibliography on or
       Related to Black Women." Journal of Social and Behavioral
       Sciences 21 (1975):90-135.
           No explanation of the scope intended for this bibliog-
       raphy is given. It is an alphabetical listing of over 650
       books, articles, and dissertations, some as early as the
       1930s, most dated since 1960. The focus appears to be on
       the behavioral sciences and medicine, but there are some
       references to belles-lettres and popular literature.

430   KLOTMAN, PHYLLIS RAUCH and BAATZ, WILMER H. The Black Family
       and the Black Woman: A Bibliography. New York: Arno
       Press, 1978. 231 pp.
           This is the revised and enlarged edition of a 1972 work
       that was also based on the holdings of the Indiana University
       Libraries, whose collections include books and articles from
       nineteenth century slave narratives to contemporary research.
       It is for the most part a subject-arranged bibliography in
       two divisions: the black family (subdivided by period, with
       a section of children's literature) and the black woman
       (subdivided topically). Under most topics there are further
       divisions by type of material, and there are supplementary
       lists of periodicals, reference books, audiocassettes,
       government publications, and ERIC documents. Entries are
       cross-listed when they are relevant to more than one topic,
       but there are no indexes.

431   McAFEE, SANDRA WRAY. "Selected Books, Articles, and Mono-
       graphs Relevant to Black Women and to Black Students in
       Higher Education." In New Research on Women and Sex Roles
       at the University of Michigan. Ed. Dorothy G. McGuigan.
       Ann Arbor: Center for Continuing Education of Women, 1976,
       pp. 322-31.
           The materials listed in this alphabetical sequence of
       over 100 titles include not only the forms stated in the
       title but also dissertations, reports, and government
       documents. Their dates cover the period from the 1920s to
       the mid-1970s.

432   MacDONALD, JOHN STUART and MacDONALD, LEATRICE. "The Black
       Family in the Americas: A Review of the Literature." Sage
       Race Relations Abstracts 3 (Feb. 1978):1-42.
           This essay reviews the scholarly literature since 1960
       dealing with the black family in the U.S., the Caribbean,
       and Latin America. The reference list contains 150 titles,
       alphabetically arranged.

433   NATIONAL URBAN LEAGUE. A Selected Annotated Bibliography on
       Black Families. Vol. 1. Washington: National Center on
       Child Abuse and Neglect; for sale by Supt. of Docs., U.S.
       Govt. Print. Off., 1978. 38 pp. Available from EDRS, ED
       156 814.
           This is a reprint of a publication developed by the
       National Urban League's Project Thrive, a demonstration
       project concerned with the delivery of child protective
       services and aimed at black parents as well as at profes-
       sionals in the field. The titles listed are largely
       scholarly writings from the behavioral sciences, with a
       few examples of black creative writing giving insight into
       family life. Arrangement is alphabetical, but since each
       entry has not only a long evaluative annotation but also
       a letter prefix keyed to a list of subjects, it is possible
       to locate items on a given subject by scanning the prefixes.

434   RUSHING, ANDREA BENTON. "An Annotated Bibliography of Images
       of Black Women in Black Literature." CLA Journal 21 (March
       1978):435-42.
           "This bibliography, which does not pretend to be exhaus-
       tive, brings together for the first time all the pertinent
       material I discovered in a thorough preliminary investiga-
       tion of books and periodicals from 1959 to 1977." The
       thirty-three works cited are concerned with African, Carib-
       bean, and Afro-American literature.

*435   Sage Race Relations Abstracts. vol. 1- 1975- Beverly Hills,
       Calif.: Sage Publications, 1975- Quarterly.
           This international abstracting journal covers books,
       scholarly and general periodicals, newspapers, and
       ephemeral community-oriented publications. Useful sections
       are Family and Adoption, and Women.

436   SCOTT, PATRICIA BELL. "A Critical Overview of Sex Role Re-
       search on Black Families." Women Studies Abstracts 5 (Summer
       1976):1-14.
           The aim of the review essay is "to discuss that litera-
       ture which related to sex role development among Blacks, to
       raise some questions concerning the process of socialization
       among Blacks, and to develop a list of research priorities."

Both the 36 References and the 84 Additional Reference
Materials and Bibliographies are alphabetical lists of
scholarly books, articles, and dissertations dated since
1965.

437   SIMS, JANET L. Black Women in the Employment Sector. Public
       Administration Series, no. P243. Monticello, Ill.: Vance
       Bibliographies, 1979. 28 pp.
           Articles from the black periodical press make up a large
       part of this bibliography, but it also includes government
       documents, scholarly and general articles, theses, dis-
       sertations, and a few books. Their dates range from the
       late nineteenth century through the mid-1970s. The unique
       feature of the work is its compilation of more than 250
       titles on black women in 25 specific occupations. There
       are also about 100 General Works tucked away alphabetically
       between Engineering and Industry.

438   STONE, PAULINE TERRELONGE and BROWN, CHERYL LUVENIA. The Black
       American Woman in the Social Science Literature. Michigan
       Occasional Paper, no. 2. Ann Arbor: Women's Studies
       Program, University of Michigan, 1978. 65 pp.
           About 800 titles on black women as the object of combined
       racism and sexism are listed alphabetically in this bibliog-
       raphy. They include popular and scholarly books and arti-
       cles, unpublished papers, speeches, newspaper articles,
       dissertations and theses, and ERIC documents, some as early
       as the first decade of this century, most of them dated
       since 1960. Because it is already widely covered, the
       black family is not dealt with exhaustively; the emphasis
       is rather on the multiple roles played by black women in
       society.

439   WILLIAMS, ORA. American Black Women in the Arts and Social
       Sciences: A Bibliographic Survey. Rev. and expanded ed.
       Metuchen, N.J.: Scarecrow Press, 1978. 197 pp.
           Attempting to counteract the oversight of the American
       black woman's contribution to American society and culture,
       this bibliography cites well over 1,200 items in a general
       listing, topically divided, and a group of individual bib-
       liographies on 17 outstanding women, some of whom worked in
       several media. Emphasis is placed on black authorship of
       works included, so that biography and criticism, for example,
       are divided into sections for titles by black women and those
       by other authors. There are also lists of audiovisual aids,
       black periodicals, and black publishing houses, as well as
       a name index.

See also: 412.

Bibliographies

Italian Women

440 CAROLI, BETTY BOYD. "Italian Women in America: Sources for
Study." Italian Americana 2 (1976):242-54.
In addition to describing primary and secondary published
sources, this bibliographic essay discusses American and
Italian statistical publications, the literary treatment
of the Italian American woman, oral history, and archives.

Latino Women

441 CABELLO-ARGANDOÑA, ROBERTO; GÓMEZ-QUIÑONES, JUAN; and DURÁN,
PATRICIA HERRERA. The Chicana: A Comprehensive Bibliographic Study. Los Angeles: Chicano Studies Center, University of California, 1975. 308 pp.
The three initial sections of this work list films,
special serials, and general readings on the Chicana. The
greater part of the nearly 500 citations are in the 15
topical sections that follow, each section further divided
by type of material: books and theses, periodical articles,
and government documents/papers. Although a number of
titles cited are in Spanish and a number date back as far
as the 1920s, most of the references are in English and of
recent date. There are long and often highly evaluative
annotations for about half the items, and author and title
indexes.

442 CHAPA, EVEY et al. La Mujer Chicana: An Annotated Bibliography. Austin, Texas: Chicana Research and Learning
Center, 1976. 94 pp. Available from EDRS, ED 152 439.
This bibliography comprises references to about 300
books, articles, government documents, and unpublished
papers in Spanish and English. They are dated between
1916 and 1975, the majority between 1960 and 1975, and
grouped in subject categories. There are no indexes, but
items related to more than one subject are cross-listed.
An appendix gives addresses for publications and organizations not readily located.

443 Hispanic Women and Education: Annotated Selected References
and Resources. Bibliography Series, no. 5. San Francisco:
Women's Educational Equity Communications Network, 1978.
15 pp. Available from WEECN, Far West Laboratory for Educational Research and Development, 1855 Folsom St., San
Francisco, CA 94103, or from EDRS, ED 164 246.
Only publications in English are listed among the eighty-
two references to publications concerned with the education
of women of Spanish origin in the U.S. The majority of the
titles are limited in scope to women of one particular

Hispanic group, most commonly Chicanas but in some cases
Puerto Ricans or Cubans. The citations are grouped by
categories reflecting format or subject matter, and a
supplementary list describes thirteen Hispanic organizations
or resource groups.

444   PORTILLO, CRISTINA; RIOS, GRACIELA, and RODRIGUEZ, MARTHA.
       Bibliography of Writings on La Mujer. Berkeley: Chicano
       Studies Library, University of California, 1976.   53 pp.
       Available from EDRS, ED 164 216.
           Materials in both English and Spanish, chiefly those
       published between the late sixties and 1976, are included
       in this bibliography based on a special Chicano library
       collection.   The first part lists 264 books, articles,
       dissertations, student papers, and documents.   Part 2
       lists nineteen periodicals specifically on Chicanas or
       likely to include a number of relevant articles.   There is
       a subject index.

Native American Women

445   MEDICINE, BEATRICE.   "The Role of Women in Native American
       Societies: A Bibliography."   Indian Historian 8 (Aug.
       1975):50-54.
           Only Native Americans north of the Rio Grande are con-
       sidered in this bibliography, the outgrowth of a course
       taught in the Native American Studies Department of
       Dartmouth College.   The list of about 100 references in-
       cludes both primary and secondary sources published as
       either books or periodical articles.

446   Native American Women: A Selected Topics Bibliography of ERIC
       Documents.   University Park: Eric Clearinghouse on Rural
       Education and Small Schools, New Mexico State University,
       1977.   42 pp.   Available from ERIC, ED 152 472.
           The topics covered in this partially annotated bibliog-
       raphy of fifty entries include role models, post-secondary
       education, employment, counseling programs, and cultural
       education.   It was produced by a search of Resources in
       Education and Current Index to Journals in Education for
       the period 1968-1976.   Arrangement is by ERIC accession
       number inverted, so that the most recent titles come first.
       Item from RIE have abstracts; those from CIJE may have no
       more annotation than the list of descriptors assigned.

Bibliographies

Age Groups

Teen Age

447 Annotated Bibliography, 1964-1974, of the Needs, Concerns and
    Aspirations of Adolescent Girls, 12-18 Years. St. Paul:
    Center for Youth Development and Research, University of
    Minnesota, 1975. 204 pp.
        The contents of this work include the entire bibliography
    from a monograph, relevant titles from Westervelt and
    Fixter (264), and other monographs and articles retrieved
    by a search of American Book Publishing Record, Disserta-
    tion Abstracts International, and the data bases for crim-
    inology, education, medicine, and psychology. The entries
    from each source are arranged in a separate section, with
    no indexes or other means of subject access.

448 KIDDER, MARY JANE. Counseling the Pregnant Teenager. Ann
    Arbor, Mich.: ERIC Clearinghouse on Counseling and Person-
    nel Services, 1971. 12 pp. Available from EDRS, ED 061
    564. Continued by:

449 KOPITA, RONALD R. Counseling the Pregnant Teenager. Ann
    Arbor, Mich.: ERIC Clearinghouse on Counseling and
    Personnel Services, 1973. 7 pp. Available from EDRS, ED
    082 105. Continued by:

450 GALANT, RICHARD and MONCRIEFF, NANCY J. Counseling the Preg-
    nant Teenager. Ann Arbor, Mich.: ERIC Clearinghouse on
    Counseling and Personnel Services, 1974. 12 pp. Available
    from EDRS, ED 105 359.
        These three bibliographies together provide substantial
    abstracts for seventy-four journal articles, ERIC documents,
    and dissertations describing attempts by school systems to
    provide the support for pregant teenagers that will prevent
    their dropping out of school.

451 NATIONAL ALLIANCE CONCERNED WITH SCHOOL AGE PARENTS. "Parenting
    Guide: Selected Resources and Materials, 1965-1975." In
    U.S. Congress. Senate. Labor and Public Welfare Committee.
    Hearings: School-Age Mother and Child Health Act, 1975.
    94th Cong., 1st sess., Nov. 4, 1975, pp. 779-878.
        Although intended for those working with adolescent
    parents and not for researchers, this compilation of nearly
    350 titles contains a number that are of research value.
    Its three main sections are concerned with the development
    of parenting skills, research and program aids, and AV and
    bibliographic aids.

452   PERKINS, BARBARA BRIDGMAN. <u>Adolescent Birth Planning and</u>
       <u>Sexuality: Abstracts of the Literature</u>. Washington:
       Consortium on Early Childbearing and Childrearing, Child
       Welfare League of America, 1974. 75 pp.
            A search of medical and social science literature for
       the period 1965-1973 produced this bibliography of scholarly
       articles, conference papers, pamphlets, and a few books.
       (Books written for adolescents or their parents were ex-
       cluded.) About 100 substantial abstracts are grouped in
       subject chapters on aspects of adolescent contraception,
       abortion, and sexual behavior. There is an author index.

453   PLIONIS, BETTY MOORE. "Adolescent Pregnancy: Review of the
       Literature." <u>Social Work</u> 20 (July 1975):302-307.
            Most of the psychological, sociological, and medical
       literature reviewed in this essay appeared in the 1960s
       and 1970s. The sixty-odd titles cited in the notes include
       unpublished theses as well as books and articles.

454   STEWART, KAREN ROBB. <u>Adolescent Sexuality and Teenage Preg-</u>
       <u>nancy: A Selected, Annotated Bibliography with Summary</u>
       <u>Forewords</u>. Chapel Hill: Carolina Population Center,
       University of North Carolina, 1976. 43 pp.
            The compiler describes this guide as designed to help
       providers of social services or the parents of adolescents
       to discriminate among the growing number of general and
       professional articles on adolescent sexuality and teenage
       pregnancy. The selection of 138 titles published chiefly
       between 1965 and 1976 represents the literature most often
       cited and most useful. Concise descriptive annotations
       are supplemented by the summary essays that preface each
       of the nine topical chapters.

Middle Age

See also the section on Employment Reentry.

455   BARNETT, ROSALIND C. and BARUCH, GRACE K. "Women in the
       Middle Years: A Critique of Research and Theory." <u>Psy-</u>
       <u>chology of Women Quarterly</u> 3 (Winter 1978):187-97.
            "Research and theory on women in the middle years
       reflect assumptions and biases that limit our understanding
       and impair our ability to resolve conflicting findings
       about women's well-being." The authors give a critical
       review of about forty published and unpublished studies
       in this area, most of them dating from the 1970s, and
       suggest areas for further research.

456   ELKIN, ANNA. <u>The Emerging Role of Mature Women, Basic Background Data in Employment and Continuing Education: A
Selected Annotated Bibliography Primarily of Free and Inexpensive Materials</u>. New York: Federation Employment and
Guidance Service, 1976. 20 pp. Available from EDRS, ED
123 415.
        Government documents, pamphlets, and periodical articles
make up the greater part of this bibliography of over 100
items published between 1969 and 1975. They deal chiefly
with the employment and vocational training of women in
general or the socioeconomic situation of older women. Only
a few titles are concerned specifically with the employment
of mature women.

457   <u>Women in Midlife--Security and Fulfillment: A Compendium of
Papers Submitted to the Select Committee on Aging and the
Subcommittee on Retirement Income and Employment, U.S.
House of Representatives, Ninety-fifth Congress, second
session, December 1978. Part 2: Annotated Bibliography</u>.
Washington: U.S. Govt. Print. Off., 1979. 181 pp.
        This extensive classified bibliography of recent
scholarly and general materials on the problems of middle-
aged women covers such topics as the displaced homemaker,
volunteer work, retirement preparation, continuing education, employment, pensions, lack of promotion, housing,
and mental health.

See also: 458, *459.

Senior Women

458   BEESON, DIANE. "Women in Studies of Aging: A Critique and
Suggestion." <u>Social Problems</u> 23 (Oct. 1975):52-59.
        The author criticizes the theoretical and methodological
assumptions of social gerontologists who, in their increas-
ing attention to female subjects, have frequently compared
their experience of aging to that of men and found it more
difficult. Feminist writings, on the other hand, point out
problems seldom mentioned in academic gerontological literature. The bibliography lists twenty-six items of both
types.

*459   <u>Current Literature on Aging</u>. vol. 1- Washington: National
Council on the Aging, 1957- Quarterly.
        This annotated bibliography of selected publications in
the field of aging and related areas is arranged under
subject terms, one of which is Women. It has an annual
index.

460   HOLLENSHEAD, CAROL. <u>Past Sixty: The Older Woman in Print and
Film</u>. Ann Arbor: Institute of Gerontology, University of
Michigan-Wayne State University, 1977. 52 pp.

This selected annotated bibliography cites 289 books, articles, pamphlets, and films. Printed materials include both scholarly and popular literature. They are listed under nine categories: social and psychological issues, marriage and extended family, widowhood, health, sexuality, legal and economic issues, ethnic background, and the humanities. A list of films and videotapes and one of distributors complete the work.

461 INTERFACE BIBLIOGRAPHERS. Age Is Becoming: An Annotated Bibliography on Women and Aging. San Francisco: Glide Publications, 1976. 36 pp. Available from Glide Publications, 330 Ellis St., San Francisco, CA 94102.
   A project of the Task Force on Older Women of the National Organization for Women, this highly selective bibliography concentrates on American material, both general and scholarly, published between 1970 and 1975. The organization is mainly by topics (role changes, sexuality, widowhood, etc.) but also includes sections of biography and fiction.

Other Social Groups

Criminals

462 DOLESCHAL, EUGENE. "The Female Offender: A Guide to Published Materials." Crime and Delinquency Literature 2 (Dec. 1970):639-69.
   The first part of this literature review is a bibliographic essay on female crime patterns and the female offender in the corrections system. It is followed by an annotated bibliography, topically arranged, of eighty references from the literature of criminology and the social sciences having to do with women criminals in North America, Britain, and western Europe.

463 GOYER-MICHAUD, FRANCYNE. "The Adult Female Offender: A Selected Bibliography." Criminal Justice and Behavior 1 (Dec. 1974):340-56.
   This is an international listing of 221 periodical articles in English or French which appeared in professional legal, medical, criminological, psychiatric, or social work journals from 1959 through 1974. The arrangement is alphabetical by author, but each citation is followed by one or more code letters indicating broad subject area or type of study.

464   KLEIN, DORIE. "The Etiology of Female Crime: A Review of
      the Literature." Issues in Criminology 8 (Fall 1973):3-30.
      Reprinted in The Female Offender. Ed. Laura Crites.
      Lexington, Mass.: Lexington Books, 1977, pp. 5-31.
           In the belief that it is necessary to understand the
      assumptions of the writers of the small body of literature
      specifically concerned with women and crime in order to do
      feminist research on the subject, Klein has selected twenty-
      seven influential or representative works dating from the
      turn of the century to the early seventies. The value of
      the essay lies not in the number of works reviewed but in
      its perspective.

465   ROSENZWEIG, MARIANNE and BRODSKY, ANNETTE M. The Psychology
      of the Female Offender: A Research Bibliography. Report
      no. 32. University: Center for Correctional Psychology,
      University of Alabama, 1976. 45 pp.
           This interdisciplinary group of readily available
      materials was selected from the correctional, psychologi-
      cal, and sociological literature published from 1950
      through August 1975 for their usefulness to behavioral
      scientists. Citations to books and journal articles are
      organized into separate sections on adult and juvenile
      offenders; each of these is further divided into sections
      on theory and on research or treatment. There are supple-
      mentary lists of dissertations and bibliographies. All the
      entries except dissertations have abstracts.

466   STURGEON, SUSAN and RANS, LAUREL. The Woman Offender: A
      Bibliographic Sourcebook. Pittsburgh: Entropy Ltd., 1975.
      63 pp. Available from Entropy Ltd., South Great Road,
      Lincoln, MA 01773.
           The writings cited in this bibliography are books,
      articles, documents, reports, dissertations, and other
      studies produced in the U.S. in the period 1965-1975. The
      work consists of an annotated bibliography of about 100
      titles and an unannotated list of over 200, each section
      further divided by type of material. A group of twenty-five
      bibliographies and literature reviews that appears only in
      the unannotated section is worth noting. An appendix
      describes projects funded by the Department of Labor and
      the Law Enforcement Assistance Administration in 1974-1975.

467   VELIMESIS, MARGERY L. "The Female Offender." Crime and
      Delinquency Literature 7 (March 1975):94-112.
           Topics covered in this review of research between 1970
      and 1975 include characteristics of women in prison, parole
      recidivism, correctional programs, images of women, the
      courts' treatment of women, and areas for further research.
      The footnotes cite about fifty studies.

Bibliographies

Disabled Women

468   <u>Disabled Women and Equal Opportunity</u>. Resource Roundup. San
       Francisco: Women's Educational Equity Communications Net-
       work, 1979. 6 pp. Available from Far West Laboratory for
       Educational Research and Development, 1855 Folsom St.,
       San Francisco, CA 94103.
           In this bibliography close to 100 print and nonprint
       materials are listed with full information for ordering
       and, where titles are not self-explanatory, brief annota-
       tions. They are grouped in broad subject categories:
       general resources, elementary/secondary education, voca-
       tional/higher education, occupational resources, health/
       sex counseling, nonprint media, media services, organiza-
       tions/resource groups. Because so few items deal solely
       with disabled women, these entries are marked.

Divorced Women

469   KESSLER, SHEILA. <u>A Divorce Bibliography</u>. 1975. 27 pp.
       Available from EDRS, ED 119 095.
           This work is made up of two selected bibliographies
       prepared for a workshop on divorce, seemingly for marriage
       counselors, given in 1975. The first, unannotated, consists
       of an alphabetical listing of about 350 entries for books,
       articles, and government documents. Publications cited are
       from the general, social science, and legal literature,
       principally since 1960, and include some references to
       divorce in countries other than the U.S. The second bib-
       liography supplies annotations for about thirty recent
       books on divorce.

470   McKENNEY, MARY. <u>Divorce: A Selected Annotated Bibliography</u>.
       Metuchen, N.J.: Scarecrow Press, 1975. 157 pp.
           The compiler states that she has chosen to include
       "every 'significant' writing on divorce in English through
       1972 I could find, as well as some items of debatable signi-
       ficance but some interest; all popular legal works and all
       statistical works I could locate; a sample of the literature
       and films dealing with divorce; and a few items published
       after 1972." Her feminist viewpoint is reflected in the
       annotations but not in the selection. The 613 entries,
       almost all of which have to do with the U.S., are arranged
       in subject categories, with the items of greatest signi-
       ficance starred. There are appendixes listing resource
       organizations and state divorce laws, as well as author
       and subject indexes.

471   SELL, KENNETH D. <u>Divorce in the 1970's: A Subject Guide to</u>
<u>Books, Articles, Dissertations, Government Documents, and</u>
<u>Film on Divorce in the United States, 1970-1976.</u> Prelim-
inary ed. Salisbury, N.C.: the author, 1977. 22 pp.
1977 supp. 14 pp. 1978 supp. 14 pp. Available from Dr.
Kenneth D. Sell, Dept. of Sociology, Catawba College,
Salisbury, N.C. 28144.
   "This bibliography deals with the social, psychological,
psychiatric, economic, legal, religious, historical, and
literary aspects of divorce and divorce related topics.
An attempt was made to find all of the books, articles,
dissertations, films and project reports published in the
United States or about divorce in the United States in this
decade. The popular and legal literature was not systemat-
ically searched." Together, the three parts cite over
1,200 items in a subject arrangement of twenty-two categories, each further divided by form of material. Additional
supplements are planned.

472   _____ and SELL, BETTY H. <u>Divorce in the United States, Canada,</u>
<u>and Great Britain: A Guide to Information Sources.</u> Detroit,
Mich.: Gale Research Co., 1978. 298 pp.
   This is not a listing of references on divorce, but
rather a guide to locating materials on the subject in a
variety of sources, specific and general. The greater part
of the book is devoted to descriptions of standard reference
tools, with suggested subject headings and brief evaluations
of the works' usefulness for research on divorce. The chief
contributions of the guide, however, are the list of nearly
200 dissertations from 1891 to 1978 and the directions for
locating divorce statistics for the U.S., Canada, and Great
Britain and divorce laws for individual states.

See also: 420.

Lesbians

473   DAMON, GENE; WATSON, JAN; and JORDAN, ROBIN. <u>The Lesbian in</u>
<u>Literature: A Bibliography.</u> 2d ed. Reno, <u>Nev.: The</u>
<u>Ladder</u>, 1975. 96 pp. Available from Naiad Press, 7800
Westside Dr., Weatherby Lake, MO 64152.
   "Gene Damon" is the pseudonym of Barbara Grier, and this
book may be found in library catalogs under that name. It
lists over 1,500 works of English language fiction, poetry,
drama, biography, or autobiography concerned with lesbianism
or having lesbian characters and published not later than
1974. A few works of nonfiction issued from 1967 through
1974 dealing with lesbianism as a subject area and considered accurate by the compilers are included. There are

only occasional annotations, but a coding system indicates
the amount of lesbian content, the quality of its treatment,
and in many cases the literary genre of a title. For a
forthcoming third edition, see 474.

474 GRIER, BARBARA et al. The Lesbian in Literature. 3d ed.
Weatherby Lake, Mo.: Naiad Press, forthcoming.
   The publisher describes this as a comprehensive bibliog-
raphy of about 7,000 entries listing "all fiction, poetry,
drama, auto and biography on the subject of Lesbians and
Lesbianism available in the English language."

475 KUDA, MARIE J. Women Loving Women. Chicago: Womanpress,
1975. 28 pp. Available from Womanpress, P.O. Box 59330,
Chicago IL 60645.
   About 200 works of fiction, poetry, biography, and autobiography in English published between 1914 and 1974 are
listed alphabetically by author in this bibliography. The
annotations evaluate titles primarily in terms of their
treatment of lesbian subject matter.

*476 Lesbian Herstory Archives News. no. 1- June 1975- Irregular.
Available from Lesbian Herstory Educational Foundation,
Inc., P.O. Box 1258, New York, N.Y. 10001.
   Each issue of this newsletter has featured a bibliography
based on the Archives's holdings on some aspect of lesbian
culture. Topics covered through the Spring 1979 issue have
included serial media, bibliographies, paperbacks from the
1930s to the 1950s, poetry , and short stories.

477 MANNION, KRISTIANN. "Female Homosexuality: A Comprehensive
Review of Theory and Research." Catalog of Selected Documents in Psychology 6 (May 1976):44. MS 1247. 95 pp.
   This extensive critical survey analyzes psychoanalytic
theories of lesbianism, empirical studies of the lesbian
personality, methodology of past and future research, biological factors in the development of lesbianism, and the
relationship of feminism and lesbianism. The accompanying
list of seventy references is drawn largely from British
and American professional psychological literature.

478 O'DONNELL, MARY. "Lesbian Health Care: Issues and Literature."
Science for the People, May/June 1978, pp. 9-19.
Reprint available from Santa Cruz Women's Health Center,
250 Locust St., Santa Cruz, CA 95060.
   This review of the scanty literature on lesbian health
issues covers the topics gynecology, medical research,
reproduction, mental health, stress, and gay health workers.
The list of forty-two references is supplemented by an
Annotated Literature List which comments on about half of
them.

479   RIESS, BERNARD F.; SAFER, JEANNE; and YOTIVE, WILLIAM. "Psychological Test Data on Female Homosexuality: A Review of
the Literature." <u>Journal of Homosexuality</u> 1 (1974):71-86.
This essay offers a "critical and comparative review
. . .of all existing studies on responses by female homo-
sexuals to projective and nonprojective tests." The
reference list cites twenty-three titles.

480   SILLMAN, AMY. "Bibliography" [on lesbian art and artists]
<u>Heresies</u> 3 (Fall 1977):115-17.
This partially annotated list of over 100 items cites
books, periodical articles, and unpublished papers in
separate sections.

See also: 369, 522.

Prostitutes

481   <u>A Bibliography of Prostitution</u>. Edited by Vern Bullough et al.
New York: Garland Publishing, 1977. 419 pp.
Comprehensive coverage is the aim of this bibliography
of nearly 6,500 books and articles in English and western
languages. Its arrangement includes divisions by literary
form (e.g., biography, fiction), broad subject (anthropology,
history), and more specific topics (legal and police regulations, war). These narrow classifications are especially
welcome because the work has only an author index.

Radical Women

482   LOADER, JAYNE. "Women in the Left, 1906-1941: A Bibliography
of Primary Sources." <u>University of Michigan Papers in
Women's Studies</u> 2 (September 1975):9-82.
"This bibliography includes an annotated selection of
primary sources by and about women in the anarchist movement, the radical culture movement centered in Greenwich
Village in the 1910s and 1920s, and the Communist Party
and its affiliates before World War II." Both published
and unpublished articles, poems, plays, short stories,
novels, and autobiographies are cited in a topical arrangement with name index. Although the principal concern is
with women of the U.S., there are small sections on the
Soviet Union, Spain, China, and France. The two appendixes
are Notes on Sources (radical periodicals and anthologies)
and Other Work by Radical Women.

Rural Women

Bibliographies concerned primarily with women in rural development
are listed in the geographical section on the Third World.

483   JOYCE, LYNDA M. and LEADLEY, SAMUEL M.   An Assessment of
      Research Needs of Women in the Rural United States: Litera-
      ture Review and Annotated Bibliography.   University Park:
      Pennsylvania Agricultural Experiment Station, Pennsylvania
      State University, 1977.   154 pp.   Available from EDRS, ED
      141 565.
         The review of research on women in rural areas of the
      U.S. from 1900 to the mid-seventies discusses methods and
      theories, needs for future research, and the present status
      of rural women.   Next, a thirty-page annotated bibliography
      covers popular literature, monographs, and agricultural
      bulletins as well as all research studies referred to in
      the review.   This alphabetically arranged bibliography is
      followed by a chronological arrangement of the same titles
      without annotations, an international bibliography, unan-
      notated, citing about seventy items in a number of languages
      published between 1967 and 1975, and a list of eleven
      periodicals concerned with rural women in the U.S.

484   MOSER, COLLETTE, and JOHNSON, DEBORAH.   Rural Women Workers in
      the 20th Century: An Annotated Bibliography.   Special
      Paper, no. 15.   East Lansing, Mich.:   Center for Rural
      Manpower and Public Affairs, Michigan State University,
      1973.   63 pp.   Available from EDRS, ED 100 570, also from
      NTIS, PB 226 487.
         Noting that only one-third of rural employment is on
      farms, this bibliography is concerned with rural women
      workers in general from 1875 to 1971, chiefly but not
      entirely in the U.S.   Its 338 entries include both research
      studies and articles from rural magazines.

485   Rural Women and Education: Annotated Selected References and
      Resources.   Bibliography Series, no. 6.   San Francisco:
      Women's Educational Equity Communications Network, 1978.
      23 pp.   Available from Far West Laboratory for Educational
      Research and Development, 1855 Folsom St., San Francisco,
      CA 94103, also from EDRS, ED 160 334.
         The Selected References are fifty-six books, articles,
      pamphlets, and ERIC documents, topically arranged.   The
      Resources are eight current periodicals and thirty-five
      organizations, agencies, or projects concerned with the
      education of rural women.   All materials are readily avail-
      able and full order information is provided.

See also: 290, 328.

      Urban Women

486   DINER, HASIA R.   Women and Urban Society: A Guide to Informa-
      tion Sources.   Detroit, Mich.:   Gale Research Co., 1979.
      138 pp.

The impact of urban life on women in the U.S., Europe, Asia, Africa, and Latin America is covered in this annotated international bibliography of scholarly publications. Most of the books, articles, dissertations, and conference papers included were published after World War II. The main body of the book is organized into six sections dealing with women and urbanization, women in urban families, urban fertility, employment of urban women, women's roles in urban society, and attitudes towards urban women. Three appendixes provide a selected bibliography of books recommended for a small library or a personal collection and lists of indexes/abstracts and periodicals relevant to the topic. There are author, title, and subject indexes.

487 LOFLAND, LYN H. "The 'Thereness' of Women: A Selective Review of Urban Sociology." Sociological Inquiry 45, nos. 2-3 (1975):144-70. Reprinted in Another Voice: Feminist Perspectives on Social Life and Social Science. Ed. Marcia Millman and Rosabeth Moss Kanter. New York: Octagon Books, 1976, pp. 144-70.
This literature review evaluates the treatment of women in empirical works of urban sociology dealing with twentieth-century Britain and the U.S. The reference list cites fifty-six titles.

Widows

488 BARRETT, CAROL J. "Review Essay: Women in Widowhood." Signs 2 (Summer 1977):856-68.
The stresses of widowhood and the implications for social policy are the subject of this literature review covering published and unpublished materials for the period 1950-1975. The footnotes cite nearly sixty titles.

489 BERARDO, FELIX M. "Widowhood Status in the United States: Perspective on a Neglected Aspect of the Family Life-Cycle." In The One-Parent Family: Perspectives and Annotated Bibliography. Ed. Benjamin Schlesinger. Toronto: University of Toronto Press, 1969, pp. 26-53.
This essay does not appear in the third edition of The One-Parent Family (420). It consists of a sociological analysis of widowhood status in the U.S. followed by a bibliography of over seventy books, articles, reports, and documents, most of them from the 1950s and 1960s.

490 HILTZ, STARR ROXANNE. "Widowhood: A Roleless Role." Marriage and Family Review 1 (Nov./Dec. 1978):1, 3-10.
"This article reviews selected works by sociologists, psychologists, and social workers on widowhood in American

society. Emphasis is upon studies which examine the
factors related to the change or dissolution of old role
relationships and their replacement by new ones; aspects
of widowhood which are related to the structure and func-
tioning of the American family as a whole; and the recent
emergence of social service programs aimed at aiding
widows in reshaping their lives and identities." Most of
the fifty-four references cited were published in the 1970s.

491 STRUGNELL, CÉCILE. <u>Adjustment to Widowhood and Some Related
Problems: A Selective and Annotated Bibliography</u>. New
York: Health Sciences Publishing, 1974. 201 pp.
     Well over 500 books and articles, including twenty other
bibliographies, are cited in this compilation. Most of
them were published before 1972. Although the introduction
states, "We have not attempted to cover literature other
than Anglo-American," there is a small section in the
topical arrangement devoted to cross-cultural studies.

See also: 420.

PSYCHOLOGY

General

492 BAER, HELEN R. and SHERIF, CAROLYN. "A Topical Bibliography
(Selectively Annotated) on the Psychology of Women."
<u>Catalog of Selected Documents in Psychology</u> 4 (Spring 1974):
42. MS 614. 112 pp.
     In this bibliography of over 1,000 entries, the books
and articles chosen for annotation are described in detail,
some of the books even chapter by chapter. Each of the
topical divisions is made up of basic readings and subsections on specialized problems. The topics covered
include historical perspectives, the contemporary women's
movement, the biological basis of sex differences, cross-
cultural perspectives, psycho-social development, cognitive
differences and achievement, sexuality and reproduction,
psycho-social problems, and aging.

493 CROMWELL, PHYLLIS E. <u>Woman and Mental Health: Selected
Annotated References, 1970-73</u>. Rockville, Md.: Division
of Scientific and Technical Information, National Institute
of Mental Health; for sale by Supt. of Docs., U.S. Govt.
Print. Off., 1974. 247 pp.
     This bibliography abstracts 810 items, primarily articles
from English-language academic and professional journals,
but also books, dissertations, and audiovisual resources.
The twenty-one broad subjects under which entries are listed

include a wide range of social groups and issues as well
as topics generally associated with mental health.

494 MACCOBY, ELEANOR EMMONS and JACKLIN, CAROL NAGY. "Annotated
     Bibliography." In The Psychology of Sex Differences.
     Stanford, Calif.: Stanford University Press, 1974, pp.
     393-697.
         The text of the book examines the nature of sex differ-
     ences, the stages of their development, and the major
     psychological theories offered in explanation. It focuses
     on childhood and adolescence but gives some attention to
     adults as well. The bibliography, which is separate from
     the book's reference list and much more extensive, covers
     research in this area published for the most part from
     1967 through 1973. The studies are grouped in subject
     categories according to types of sex differences or puta-
     tive causes.

495 MEDNICK, MARTHA T.S. and WEISSMAN, HILDA J. "The Psychology
     of Women: Selected Topics." Annual Review of Psychology
     26 (1975):1-18.
         The areas of research chosen for consideration in this
     survey are sex roles, achievement motivation, and the
     impact of feminist thought and knowledge about female
     sexuality on theories and practice in psychotherapy.

496 PARLEE, MARY BROWN. "The Premenstrual Syndrome." Psycholog-
     ical Bulletin 80 (Dec. 1973):454-65.
         This article reviews medical and psychological litera-
     ture on the psychological changes associated with the
     menstrual cycle commonly referred to as the premenstrual
     syndrome. The list of references cites seventy-two British
     and American publications dated from 1931 through 1972.

497 _____. "Review Essay: Psychology." Signs 1 (Autumn 1975):
     119-38.
         Research and bibliographic resources for the period from
     1970 to mid-1975 are covered in this survey. It is divided
     into sections dealing with traditional research on the
     psychology of women, studies pointing out the inadequacies
     of such psychology, and research conducted by feminist
     psychologists. The references appear only as footnotes.

498 SEIDEN, ANNE M. "Overview: Research on the Psychology of
     Women. I. Gender Differences and Sexual and Reproductive
     Life." American Journal of Psychiatry 133 (Sept. 1976):
     995-1007.
         This review essay features the major works of recent
     research in the areas of sex differences, menstrual cycle,
     menopause, diseases of the reproductive organs, coitus,
     rape, childbirth, and fertility control, with an evaluation

of the limitations and significance of the data. The
bibliography cites 132 writings from women's studies and
professional literature.

499 _____. _____. "II. Women in Families, Work, and Psycho-
therapy." American Journal of Psychiatry 133 (Oct. 1976):
1111-23.
This article reviews recent research on family structure
and child-rearing, women at work, women's friendships and
love between women, clinical treatment, and effects of the
women's movement. The bibliography cites 122 titles from
both professional and social science literature.

500 SHERMAN, JULIA ANN. On the Psychology of Women: A Survey of
Empirical Studies. Springfield, Ill.: Charles C. Thomas,
1971. 304 pp. Bibliography: pp. 247-96.
The text of this work is a book-length literature review
of empirical research on the psychology of women. Its
bibliography lists well over 800 titles.

501 VAUGHTER, REESA M. "Review Essay: Psychology." Signs 2
(Autumn 1976):120-46.
"A Selected Guide to the Literature" makes up the
greater part of this essay, followed by an analysis of
contemporary feminist perspectives in psychology. The
literature review considers publications of the 1970s,
chiefly 1974-1976, on sex differences and gender roles,
psychosexuality, achievement motivation, and psychotherapy.
Citations appear only in the 122 footnotes, some of which
list several titles.

See also: 285, 522.

Achievement

502 LENNEY, ELLEN. "Women's Self-Confidence in Achievement
Settings." Psychological Bulletin 84 (Jan. 1977):1-13.
This literature review evaluates the suggestion of
previous reviewers that women display lower self-confidence
in almost all achievement situations. The author concludes
that the literature indicates this is less common than
believed and that it depends on variables that should be
more precisely identified in further research. The references list forty-one studies, almost all published since
1965.

503 O'LEARY, VIRGINIA E. "Some Attitudinal Barriers to Occupational
Aspirations in Women." Psychological Bulletin 81 (Nov.
1974):809-26.

Focus of this literature review is on attitudinal barriers that may inhibit a woman worker from engaging in the sort of achievement-oriented behavior necessary for promotion to managerial positions. Both external factors, such as the attitudes of male promoters or myths regarding women's competence and commitment, and internal factors, such as role conflict and achievement motivation, are considered. More than 120 studies, most of them published after 1960, are cited in the reference list.

504   TRESEMER, DAVID. "Research on Fear of Success: Full Annotated Bibliography." Catalog of Selected Documents in Psychology 6 (May 1976):38-39. MS 1237. 185 pp.
       The largest part of this guide to the psychological literature on fear of success is made up of detailed analyses of all 155 known research studies on the subject. This is prefaced by an account of the research tradition and methods underlying Matina Horner's classic study and followed by a review essay on research that has cited Horner's work, with a list of the more than seventy references mentioned in the essay.

Language and Nonverbal Communication

505   BAIRD, JOHN E., Jr. "Sex Differences in Group Communication: A Review of Relevant Research." Quarterly Journal of Speech 62 (Feb. 1976):179-92.
       A systematic review of psychological, sociological, educational, and professional speech literature since 1950 produced this essay. The studies described include books, journal articles, and dissertations concerned with both group behavior and other situations having implications for group communication. Citations appear only in footnotes.

506   BLAHNA, LORETTA J. A Survey of the Research on Sex Differences in Nonverbal Communication. 1975. 13 pp. Available from EDRS, ED 112 450.
       This conference paper reviews recent research on both "the observable differences in men's and women's nonverbal communication and differences in perception or evaluation when men and women are engaged in the same behavior." References are given only as notes.

507   HENLEY, NANCY and THORNE, BARRIE. "Sex Differences in Language, Speech, and Nonverbal Communication: An Annotated Bibliography." In Language and Sex: Difference and Dominance. Rowley, Mass.: Newbury House, 1975, pp. 204-311. Reprinted as She Said/He Said: An Annotated Bibliography of Sex Differences in Language, Speech, and Nonverbal Communication. Pittsburgh: KNOW, 1975, pp. 205-311.

This abstract bibliography cites about 150 items in a detailed topical arrangement covering both language about the sexes (sexist bias) and differences between the sexes in language acquisition, ability, and use, and in nonverbal communication. The titles included represent published and unpublished writings from scholarly, general, and feminist sources; most are dated since the late sixties. There is no index, but there are generous cross-references.

508 JONAS, DORIS F. and JONAS, A. DAVID. "Gender Differences in Mental Function: A Clue to the Origin of Language." <u>Current Anthropology</u> 16 (Dec. 1975):626-30.
This literature review evaluates thirty-eight scholarly British and American studies published between 1932 and 1974. The essay is organized under the headings Gender Differences in Mental Function, Evolution of the Vocal Apparatus, Circumstances Promoting the Use of Proto-Language, and Lateralization.

509 KEY, MARY RITCHIE. "Bibliography." In <u>Male/Female Language</u>, <u>with a Comprehensive Bibliography</u>. Metuchen, N.J.: Scarecrow Press, 1975, pp. 169-90.
This comprehensive alphabetical listing of about 250 books, articles, and papers on the linguistic behavior of men and women also includes some items on sociolinguistics and nonverbal communication as well as a few general titles chosen for their influence. The works cited range in date from the late nineteenth century to 1975.

510 KRAMER, CHERIS; THORNE, BARRIE; and HENLEY, NANCY. "Review Essay: Perspectives on Language and Communication." <u>Signs</u> 3 (Spring 1978):638-51.
The topics covered by this essay reviewing research since 1975 include sex differences and similarities in language use, sexism in language, relations between language structure and use, and efforts for change. Works are cited only in the fifty-eight footnotes.

511 NELSON, AUDREY A. <u>Sex and Proxemics: An Annotated Bibliography</u>. 1978. 27 pp. Available from EDRS, ED 154 454.
The focus of this bibliography is on sex differences and similarities in physical distance and body orientation. It contains over ninety titles dated from 1965 through 1977, including dissertations, articles from social psychology and communications journals, some unpublished papers, and tests.

See also: 241.

Mathematics Learning

512 ERNEST, JOHN. "Mathematics and Sex." <u>American Mathematical
Monthly</u> 83 (Oct. 1976):595–614.
The references at the close of this survey article list
eighty-one books and periodical articles. Most are of
recent date but some are as early as the 1890s.

513 FENNEMA, ELIZABETH. "Mathematics Learning and the Sexes: A
Review." <u>Journal for Research in Mathematics Education</u> 5
(May 1974):126–39.
This literature review uses tables to summarize studies
of sex differences in mathematics achievement for preschool,
early and upper elementary, and high school groups. The
bibliography cites forty-six publications.

514 FOX, LYNN; FENNEMA, ELIZABETH; and SHERMAN, JULIA. <u>Women and
Mathematics: Research Perspectives for Change.</u> Papers in
Education and Work, no. 8. Washington: National Institute
of Education, 1977. 206 pp.
Three surveys of current research on women and mathematics
achievement review different aspects of the topic. Fox
considers the effects of sex role socialization, Fennema
the influences of selected cognitive, affective, and educational variables, and Sherman the effects of biological
factors. Each paper has a list of 100–200 references,
with little duplication between lists.

Therapy and Counseling

515 CAREY, EMILY A.; MURPHY, BIANCA M.; and WASSERMAN, CHARLOTTE.
<u>Counseling Women: A Bibliography.</u> Boston: Womanspace,
1975. 12 pp. Available from Womanspace: Feminist Therapy
Collective, 636 Beacon St., Boston, MA 02215.
The special value of this alphabetical list of about
150 items lies in its inclusion of many unpublished or
fugitive materials from feminist sources.

516 CAREY, EMILY A. <u>Issues in the Psychology and Counseling of
Women: Additional Sources.</u> Boston: Womanspace, 1976.
19 pp. [For address <u>see</u> 515]
This supplement to 515 cites about 150 titles. Except
for separate lists on women and alcoholism, and lesbians
and mental health, its arrangement is unclassified.

517 _____. <u>Women: Sexuality, Psychology and Psychotherapy: A
Bibliography.</u> Boston: Womanspace, 1976. 29 pp. [For
address <u>see</u> 515]

Issued as a second supplement to 515, this list contains about 300 items, unclassified except for a separate section on sexuality.

518 HARWAY, MICHELE; ASTIN, HELEN S.; and SUHR, JEANNE M. "Selected Annotated Bibliography on Counseling Women." Catalog of Selected Documents in Psychology 7 (May 1977): 55. MS 1497. 74 pp.
Abstracts are supplied for 136 books, journal articles, papers, and pamphlets, chiefly from the 1970s. Although they are arranged alphabetically, subject access is provided by the keywords that precede each citation and give clues to the item's content.

519 MIDLARSKY, ELIZABETH. "Women, Psychopathology and Psycho-therapy: A Partially Annotated Bibliography." Catalog of Selected Documents in Psychology 7 (May 1977):41. MS 1472. 120 pp.
This bibliography contains about 1,000 references on mental health problems of women (including some fiction), therapies for women, and women as mental health profession-als. Citations are topically arranged and are chosen to represent current viewpoints from medicine, education, sociology, and corrections, as well as the literature of psychology. Most of the mateerials date from 1965-1976, but a few earlier titles of significant influence are included.

520 ZUKERMAN, ELYSE. Changing Directions in the Treatment of Women: A Mental Health Bibliography. Rockville, Md.: National Institute of Mental Health; for sale by Supt. of Docs., U.S. Govt. Print. Off., 1979. 494 pp.
From the extensive theoretical and research literature engendered by recent criticism of traditional mental health services to women, 407 titles were selected to provide a comprehensive view of the treatment of women from 1960 through winter 1977. Studies of the social situations affecting women's mental health and efforts to help them cope with the problems arising from their position in our culture are included, as are some sex-biased studies chosen to give a broad perspective. (The essay-length abstracts refrain from evaluation or comment.) References are organized into six main chapters, each extensively subdivided, and there are author and subject indexes.

HEALTH AND REPRODUCTION

<u>General</u>

521   COWAN, BELITA. <u>Women's Health Care: Resources, Writings,
       Bibliographies</u>. Ann Arbor, Mich.: Anshen Publishing,
       1978. 57 pp. Available from Belita Cowan, Anshen Pub-
       lishing, 3821 T St. NW., Washington, DC 20007.
           This is a collection of twenty essays on issues relating
       to women's physical or mental health, chiefly concerned
       with specific medical problems (e.g., sterilization abuse,
       alcohol, synthetic estrogens) but also touching on such
       issues as patient rights, doing one's own medical research,
       and women in the health professions. Each has a bibliog-
       raphy of from 30 to 100 titles selected from medical,
       general, and feminist sources. The work concludes with
       lists of recommended publications (mostly periodicals) and
       films and a directory of organizations.

522   HENEFIN, MARY SUE. "Bibliography: Women, Science, and Health."
       In <u>Women Look at Biology Looking at Women: A Collection of
       Feminist Critiques</u>. Ed. Ruth Hubbard, Mary Sue Henefin,
       and Barbara Fried. Boston: G.K. Hall; Cambridge:
       Schenkman Publishing Co., 1979, pp. 213-68.
           This introductory bibliography concentrates on readily
       available works but also includes a few less accessible
       titles of historical significance. Particularly useful
       books and review articles are starred. The arrangement is
       by subject in three principal sections. Women and Science
       includes both scientific studies of women (evolution,
       primate studies, sex differences, and the like) and writings
       on women in the scientific professions. Women and Health
       covers specific topics related to physical and mental health
       as well as women in the medical profession. A final section
       lists bibliographies and periodicals.

523   RUZEK, SHERYL K. <u>Women and Health Care: A Bibliography with
       Selected Annotation</u>. Occasional Papers, no. 1. Evanston,
       Ill.: Program on Women, Northwestern University, 1975.
       76 pp.
           Feminist and social science resources rather than pro-
       fessional medical literature are the concern of this bib-
       liography. It opens with a bibliographical essay, followed
       by the only annotated section, Women's Health Care--Basic
       Issues from a Feminist Perspective. The sections that
       follow are titled Women's Health Care Issues, Sexuality
       and Mental Health, Women's Clinics and Health Projects,
       The Social Context of Women's Health; Illness Behavior,
       Comparative Studies--Health Care in a Broader Perspective,
       Source Material on Women's Health Issues.

524 Women and the Health System: Selected Annotated References.
     Health Planning Bibliography Series, no. 4. Rockville,
     Md.: National Health Planning Information Center, 1978.
     57 pp. Available from NTIS, HRP 0300401.
          Substantial abstracts are provided for 118 publications
     from health sciences, social sciences, and women's movement
     literature issued between 1970 and March 1977. The organi-
     zation reflects women's roles as health care consumers, as
     paid health care providers, as paid decision-makers, and
     as extra-market health care providers. A final section is
     devoted to other bibliographies and periodicals. There is
     an author index.

                                            See also: 114, 367, 478.

     Fertility and Contraception

525 ASCÁDI, GYÖRGY T. A Selected Bibliography of Works on
     Fertility. World Fertility Survey Occasional Papers, no.
     10. Voorburg, Netherlands: International Statistical
     Institute, 1974. 98 pp.
          Prepared for the training of personnel for the World
     Fertility Survey, this bibliography describes at length
     selected books and articles published from 1960 through
     mid-1973. It chief value lies not in the English-language
     publications that make up the greater part of the work but
     in the smaller French and Spanish sections. References are
     organized in a topical arrangement with an author index.

526 BIRDSALL, NANCY. "Review Essay: Women and Population
     Studies." Signs 1 (Spring 1976):699-712.
          This literature review on relations between "the woman
     issue" and population reflects the author's interest in
     "the economic problems of the developing world and in
     scholarly work that is policy relevant." The footnotes
     cite about fifty published and unpublished studies dated
     between 1965 and 1975.

*527 Current Literature in Family Planning: A Monthly Classified
     Review of the Literature in the Field of Family Planning.
     New York: Katharine Dexter McCormick Library, Planned
     Parenthood World Population Information and Education Dept.,
     April 1972- Monthly.
          Each issue consists of two parts: Books (briefly
     described) and Articles (abstracted). Both sections are
     arranged by the Library's own classification system.
     Reprints or copies of articles listed are available at cost
     from the Library. The work is strongest in medical litera-
     ture but also includes the social sciences and religious
     or ethical views. Although focus is on the U.S., materials
     on other countries are listed when they are of general
     interest. Unfortunately, this tool is useful for current
     awareness only since it has no cumulations or index.

528   DAVIS, LENWOOD G. <u>The History of Birth Control in the United</u>
       <u>States: A Working Bibliography</u>. Exchange Bibliography
       861. Monticello, Ill.: Council of Planning Librarians,
       1975. 18 pp.
            In this bibliography about 200 entries are arranged by
       format: Bibliographies, Addresses/Essays/Lectures, Govern-
       ment Documents, Congresses, Books. Only the section on
       congresses is annotated.

529   _____. <u>World Population Control: A Bibliography of Selected</u>
       <u>Countries</u>. Exchange Bibliography 860. Monticello, Ill.:
       Council of Planning Librarians, 1975. 12 pp.
            The selected countries are not stated, but the intro-
       duction says that the intent is "to list only those foreign
       standard works that could be found in many of the libraries
       in the United States." Citations to about 150 books in
       English and western European languages, most of them pub-
       lished since 1950, are arranged in an alphabetical sequence.

530   FREEDMAN, RONALD. <u>The Sociology of Human Fertility: An An-</u>
       <u>notated Bibliography</u>. New York: Irvington Publishers,
       1975. 283 pp.
            Continuing an earlier bibliography covering writings up
       to 1961 (<u>Current Sociology</u> 10/11, no. 2, 1961-62), this
       work describes 1,657 English-language publications issued
       between 1961 and June 1970, with an appendix of 430 unan-
       notated citations to items published between mid-1970 and
       April 1972. Arrangement is by topical subject with a
       geographical index.

*531   GOODE, STEPHEN H. <u>Population and the Population Explosion:</u>
       <u>A Bibliography for 1970-</u> Troy, N.Y.: Whitston Publishing
       Co., 1973- Annual.
            This interdisciplinary bibliography is produced by
       searching twenty or more indexes and catalogs representing
       general, medical, legal, religious, and social science
       literature. Because most of these indexes concentrate on
       British or American publications, only for medical topics
       is it the world bibliography it aims to be. (Titles not
       originally in English are translated.) A typical volume
       contains about thirty pages of books, reports, documents,
       and pamphlets in alphabetical order by author, 150 pages
       of periodical articles listed alphabetically by title, and
       the same articles (but not the books) rearranged under
       nearly 100 subject terms. The author index applies to both
       books and articles.

532   <u>International Family-Planning Programs, 1966-1975: A Bibliog-</u>
       <u>raphy</u>. Ed. Katherine Ch'iu Lyle and Sheldon J. Segal.
       University: University of Alabama Press, 1977. 207 pp.

This is a compilation of more than 1,600 references to
"sociological, medical and behavioral literature, including
books, chapters of books, conference papers, and journal
articles, published in the English language" within the
period stated. The geographical arrangement covers eighty
countries or areas, and there are author and subject
indexes.

533   PIEPMEIER, K. B. and ADKINS, T. S. "The Status of Women and
       Fertility." Journal of Biosocial Science 5, no. 2 (1973):
       507-20.
           This literature review considers the relationship between
       fertility and education, employment, and conjugal relation-
       ship. A number of both highly developed and developing
       countries are mentioned, but the forty-one items cited are
       all in English.

534   SHARMA, PRAKASH C. Family Planning Programs: A Selected
       International Research Bibliography. Exchange Bibliography
       556. Monticello, Ill.: Council of Planning Librarians,
       1974. 21 pp.
           The principal value of this compilation of over 200
       citations to books, articles, reports, conference papers,
       and other publications lies in its inclusion of considerable
       material on Third World countries. The items listed are
       all in English and were published between 1968 and 1973.
       Organization is by type of material in seven sections.

                                        *See also: 092, *403, 452.*

Abortion

535   DOLLEN, CHARLES. Abortion in Context: A Select Bibliography.
       Metuchen, N.J.: Scarecrow Press, 1970. 150 pp.
           The emphasis of this bibliography is on the "cultural
       and philosophical aspects of abortion" and its social
       context rather than on professional medical literature.
       About 1,400 reasonably available books and articles written
       in English, mostly in the late sixties, are listed in one
       alphabetical sequence with a subject index.

*536   FLOYD, MARY K. Abortion Bibliography for 1970- Troy, N.Y.:
       Whitston Publishing Co., 1972- Annual.
           Comprehensive coverage is the intent of this bibliography
       produced by a search of more than twenty general, legal,
       and medical indexes and abstracting services. Recent
       volumes have consisted of a brief list of books, arranged
       by author, a list of well over 1,000 periodical articles,
       arranged by title, and the same articles organized under
       more than 200 subject headings. There is an author index.

537   MOORE-CAVAR, EMILY CAMPBELL.   International Inventory of
      Information on Induced Abortion.   New York: International
      Institute for the Study of Human Reproduction, Columbia
      University, 1974.   654 pp.
          This compendium attempts to assembly and summarize
      literature from all countries on all aspects of abortion.
      Data are presented in tabular form as well as in the text,
      and the lists of sources for the tables make up a valuable,
      if unconventional, international bibliography.

538   SHUSTERMAN, LISA ROSEMAN.   "The Psychosocial Factors of the
      Abortion Experience: A Critical Review."   Psychology of
      Women Quarterly 1 (Fall 1976):79-106.
          This comprehensive review evaluates the quality of
      research on a number of abortion issues: the demographic
      characteristics and motivation of women seeking abortion,
      the reasons for unwanted pregnancies, public opinion of
      abortion, and the medical and psychological consequences
      of abortion.   The list of references cites nearly 100 pub-
      lished and unpublished materials from 1940 to 1975.

Pregnancy and Childbirth

Bibliographies on teenage pregnancy are listed in the section on
Teen Age Women, under Age Groups.

539   DEVITT, NEAL.   "The Statistical Case for Elimination of the
      Midwife: Fact versus Prejudice, 1890-1935.   Part 1."
      Women and Health 4 (Spring 1979):81-86.
          "The medical literature from 1890 to 1935 that examines
      the 'midwife problem' in the United States is reviewed to
      evaluate the arguments of that period urging the elimination
      of midwifery."   The list of sixty-two references includes
      both the medical literature itself and historical or other
      secondary treatments of the topic.

540   MILLER, RITA SEIDEN.   The Social Aspects of Pregnancy: A
      Preliminary Bibliography.   Pittsburgh: KNOW, 1974.   28 pp.
          The literature of both medicine and the social sciences
      for the period 1960-1974 is represented in this alphabetical
      compilation of about 450 citations.   Since it is concerned
      strictly with pregnancy, related issues such as abortion or
      childbirth are excluded unless they are discussed in rela-
      tion to pregnancy.

541   SCHUELER, HANNELORE.   "Natural Childbirth: An Annotated Bib-
      liography."   Bulletin of Bibliography 33 (July/Sept. 1976):
      149-61.

Books and articles published between 1950 and 1975 are grouped separately in each of the three major sections: Physical Aspects of Pregnancy; Psychological Aspects of Natural Childbirth; Theory, History, and Methods of Natural Childbirth. Three appendixes list free or inexpensive materials, further sources of information, and regional directors of the International Childbirth Education Association.

542   WERTZ, RICHARD W. and WERTZ, DOROTHY C. "Bibliography." In Lying-In: A History of Childbirth in America. New York: Free Press, 1977, pp. 249-55.

This bibliographic essay evaluates and describes about seventy-five titles from the sixteenth century to the present day within the categories Histories of Birth and Obstetrics, Popular Manuals of Advice, Religion and Magic, Demography, Vital Statistics, Professionalism in Medicine and Birth Attendance, Medical Attitudes toward Women, Birth Control, Recent Comparative Studies of Childbirth.

Alcohol, Tobacco, and Drugs

543   BECKMAN, LINDA J. "The Psychosocial Characteristics of Alcoholic Women." Drug Abuse and Alcoholism Review 1 (Sept./Dec. 1978):1, 3-12.

Recent English-language scientific research on the social and psychological aspects of alcoholism in women is the subject of this review essay. Although the primary emphasis is on women in the U.S., the list of close to 100 references includes a few studies concerned with British women.

544   _____. "Women Alcoholics: A Review of Social and Psychological Studies." Journal of Studies on Alcohol 36 (July 1975):819-24.

The scope of this literature review includes "research on social-history variables, personality characteristics, social roles and role confusion, and possible treatment methods for women alcoholics." All of the 109 studies evaluated were published after 1950 and all but one are in English. Especially useful are the descriptions of four other literature reviews and their areas of concentration.

545   BOWKER, LEE H. Drug Use Among American Women, Old and Young: Sexual Oppression and Other Themes. San Francisco: R & E Research Associates, 1977. 96 pp.

Although this book is not intended to serve primarily as a bibliographic tool, a large part of the text is given over to reviewing the more significant literature published

since 1960 on female use of legal and illegal drugs.
Separate chapters deal with such topics as alcoholism and
narcotic addiction among women, males as carriers of drug
use to females, and housewife drug problems. The concluding
bibliography lists alphabetically the more than 200 titles
mentioned in the text.

546 _____. "An Introduction and Bibliographical Guide to the
Literature on Female Drug Use." Women Studies Abstracts
5 (Winter 1976):1-18.
 "In this bibliography, the field of female drug use is
defined as including alcohol, nicotine, prescription drugs,
over-the-counter preparations, and all drugs obtained on
the street." Each of its seven topical chapters is made up
of 50 to 75 citations for publications or unpublished papers,
prefaced by a brief literature review featuring outstanding
examples among the works cited. The titles listed were
chosen from medical, social science, or general sources,
with little from the field of criminology. Most of them
appeared after 1970.

547 CUSKEY, WALTER R.; BERGER, LISA H.; and DENSEN-GERBER,
JUDIANNE. "Issues in the Treatment of Female Addiction:
A Review and Critique of the Literature." Contemporary
Drug Problems 6 (Fall 1977):307-71.
 The topics around which this literature review is organized are the incidence of female addiction, recruitment of
addicts for treatment, their entry and retention, program
efficacy, and the need for a conceptual model of female
addiction. The notes cite over 100 examples of published
research in law, medicine, and the behavioral sciences.

548 EDWARDS, PATRICIA; HARVEY, CHERYL; and WHITEHEAD, PAUL C.
"Wives of Alcoholics: A Critical Review and Analysis."
Quarterly Journal of Studies on Alcohol 34 (March 1973):
112-32.
 This article reviews the literature on the personality
structure and characteristics of alcoholics' wives under
three headings: the disturbed personality theory, the
stress theory, and the psychosocial theory. The reference
list cites forty titles from the behavioral sciences.

549 GREEN, DEIDRE E. and MACDONALD, MAGGIE. Women and Psychoactive
Drug Use: An Interim Annotated Bibliography. Toronto:
Addiction Research Foundation of Ontario, 1976. 177 pp.

550 ISSEL, SUSAN M. et al. <u>Women and Alcohol: A Selective An-</u>
<u>notated Bibliography</u>. Berkeley: Social Research Group,
School of Public Health, University of California, 1976.
84 pp. Reprinted in U.S. Congress. Senate. Labor and
Public Welfare Committee. <u>Hearings: Alcohol Abuse among</u>
<u>Women: Special Problems and Unmet Needs, 1976</u>. 94th Cong.,
2d sess., Sept. 29, 1976, pp. 241-328.
      Prepared for the California Office of Alcoholism as "a
compilation of reference material dealing with alcohol
related attitudes and the drinking behavior and problems
of women and, in particular, of women in the State of
California," this bibliography supplies extensive abstracts
for about 200 books and articles, most of them published
since 1960.

551 NATIONAL CLEARINGHOUSE FOR DRUG ABUSE INFORMATION. <u>Women and</u>
<u>Drugs: An Annotated Bibliography</u>. Rockville, Md.: Na-
tional Institute on Drug Abuse, 1975. 62 pp.
      This is an update of a bibliography prepared in 1974
by the Student Association for the Study of Hallucinogens
(STASH). It cites 181 titles, most of them recent, in a
subject arrangement that includes women and narcotics,
psychotherapeutic drugs, and alcohol. There is an author
index.

Industrial Medicine

552 HUNT, VILMA R. <u>The Health of Women at Work</u>. Occasional
Papers, no. 2. Evanston, Ill.: Program on Women, North-
western University, 1977. 173 pp.
      Although its scope is limited to physical health and
a large proportion of the items listed are drawn from
medical literature, this bibliography is intended for
social scientist and historians of women as well as for
epidemiologists and clinicians. Each of the seventeen
subject chapters opens with a bibliographic essay and is
divided into English and foreign-language sources. Foreign
titles are translated. Besides sections on specific physical problems such as the effects of noise or radiation,
there are others on the history of working women, general
epidemiological studies, occupational health services, and
publications of the U.S. government and the International
Labour Office.

SPORTS

553   EIDE, MARGARET. Women and Sports: A Bibliography of Materials
      Available in the Eastern Michigan University Center of
      Educational Resources. Bibliography Series, no. 38.
      Ypsilanti: Eastern Michigan University, 1978. 41 pp.
      Available from EDRS, ED 156 631.
          Most of the materials cited in this bibliography are
      recent articles from general and physical education period-
      icals, but ERIC documents, government publications, and a
      few books are also included. The detailed subject arrange-
      ment makes it easy to locate writings on a specific topic.
      The main divisions, all much subdivided, deal with women in
      professional sports and amateur athletics, physical educa-
      tion and intramural sports, physiological and psychological
      aspects of women athletes, and equality for women in sports.

554   Girls and Women in Sports. Resource Roundup. San Francisco:
      Women's Educational Equity Communications Network, 1979.
      6 pp. Available from Far West Laboratory for Educational
      Research and Development, 1855 Folsom St., San Francisco,
      CA 94103.
          This annotated bibliography lists about seventy-five
      currently available books, periodicals, reports, ERIC
      documents, nonprint materials, and national organizations
      dealing with "the participation of girls and women in
      sports and with sports issues in schools and colleges."
      Since a large number of the publications come from non-
      commercial publishers, the inclusion of full order in-
      formation is especially useful.

555   NATIONAL ASSOCIATION FOR GIRLS AND WOMEN IN SPORT. Research
      Committee. Bibliography of Research Involving Female
      Subjects: A Compilation of Theses and Dissertations in
      Physical Education, Health, and Recreation. Ed. Waneen
      Wyrick Spirduso. Washington: American Alliance for Health,
      Physical Education, and Recreation, 1974. 212 pp.
          This nearly comprehensive listing (only two significant
      universities are not included) covers the period 1943-1972.
      Since participating institutions were asked to cite theses
      and dissertations in physical education written by women
      as well as those related to women and exercise or sport,
      some titles deal with both men and women. Citations are
      listed within subject categories that include psychological
      and physiological studies, particular sports, physical
      education for the handicapped, health, teaching methods
      and administration, and recreation.

556 Sex Discrimination in Athletics, Title IX of the Education
  Act of 1972: A Selected List of Readings. Library Bibliography Series, no. 2. Orlando: Florida Technological
  University Library, 1976. 6 pp.
    The seventy-six entries in this bibliography are arranged
  in three sections: articles from general, legal, and education periodicals; ERIC documents; U.S. government publications.

557 Women's Athletics. Bibliographies on Educational Topics, no.
  2. Washington: ERIC Clearinghouse on Teacher Education,
  1976. 43 pp. Available from EDRS, ED 130 991.
    This annotated list of nearly 100 references is the
  result of a search of the ERIC data base for an unspecified
  period, seemingly 1966-1975. It therefore consists largely
  of journal articles and educational publications not commercially available. The subject categories used include
  sex discrimination, professional associations, physical
  characteristics and performance skills, psychology and
  sociology, programs and guides, administration, history,
  and injuries.

See also: 252.

Personal Name Index

References Are To Item Numbers

Index